FROM COAST TO COAST

John A. Williams visited hotels, motels, restaurants, theaters, garages, filling stations, army bases, newspaper offices. In Wyoming his credit card was covertly checked; in Kansas City he was insulted by a hotel clerk; suspicious police cars followed his station wagon along public highways; a famous southern restaurant refused him admittance but sent a gourmet dinner to his rooming house. So it went across the country—rejection, restriction, even danger.

But there were places of promise. Warm hospitality and full acceptance greeted the Negro stranger in Denver, Louisville, Atlanta, and other isolated spots. Williams writes it all down, with a bitter honesty and with tenacious hope.

"Williams' reasoned, often poetic voice is remarkably modulated even when raised in anger . . . I enjoyed traveling with him, and I learned a number of things along the way."—The Reporter

"It is a moving book."—Virginia Kirkus

"Williams' book is done in a cool and civilized tone which makes his revelations all the more embarrassing to whites."—New York Post

Other SIGNET Books on Race Relations

THIS
IS MY
COUNTRY
TOO

John A. Williams

A SIGNET BOOK

Published by The New American Library,
New York and Toronto
The New English Library Limited, London

To
William Chiles, a friend and teacher

Copyright © 1964, 1965, BY JOHN A. WILLIAMS

FIRST PRINTING, JULY, 1966

Portions of this book originally appeared in *Holiday* Magazine, published by The Curtis Publishing Company.

SIGNET TRADEMARK REG. U.S. PAT. OFF. AND FOREIGN COUNTRIES
REGISTERED TRADEMARK—MARCA REGISTRADA
HECHO EN CHICAGO, U.S.A.

SIGNET BOOKS are published *in the United States* by
The New American Library, Inc.,
1301 Avenue of the Americas, New York, New York 10019,
in Canada by The New American Library of Canada Limited,
295 King Street East, Toronto 2, Ontario,
in the United Kingdom by The New English Library Limited,
Barnard's Inn, Holborn, London, E.C. 1, England

ACKNOWLEDGMENTS

I want to thank for help or interest in *This Is My Country Too* Harry Sions, Al Farnsworth, Harry Nickles, and many other people who were or still are on the *Holiday* staff. And Carol Brandt and the people in her agency. Thanks also are due to many people who did not appear in the text, including Dr. Charles Boseman, Ypsilanti, Michigan; the airmen at the Grand Forks, North Dakota, Strategic Air Command base; Mr. and Mrs. William Worden, Seattle, Washington; Mrs. Peg Bracken, Portland, Oregon; Mary Carter, Santa Rosa, California; and Mr. and Mrs. Kenneth Jellin, San Francisco, California. Also, James Feibleman and Shirley Ann Grau and John B. Armant of New Orleans. There are many others.

Most of all I owe a great deal of thanks to the people who took the time to write to me after publication of *This Is My Country Too* in *Holiday*. That correspondence supported my deep conviction that an afterword, written a year later, not only was warranted but also was necessary for the people who wrote, but mostly, of course, for myself.

FOREWORD

When the *Holiday* assignment to do *This Is My Country Too* was first offered to me, my impulse was not to do it. At that point no title had been suggested; I was just to drive around the country and see and listen to Americans. I was to take the pulse of the country as nearly as I could. But I told my literary agent that I didn't think it was such a good idea, especially since I had already reserved passage for an extended tour abroad. I had packed and made plans to sublet my apartment in New York.

On an August night, my reservations still intact, my bags labeled and half packed, I met with Carl D. Brandt, Jr., my agent, and Harry Sions, Editorial Director of *Holiday*. We met at the St. Regis for drinks and preliminary conversations. I had been there only once before, when, as an executive secretary for SANE, I picked up former Governor and Republican Presidential candidate Alfred M. Landon and took him to the Barry Gray Show for a broadcast. On this, my second, visit to the St. Regis, glancing about the room, I could see that of all the people in the cocktail lounge, I was the only Negro, that is, of color. I didn't have any reaction to this observation except that I remember I made it.

From the St. Regis we journeyed up to Harlem and Frank's Restaurant for dinner, and when that was finished, we went to the Red Rooster, some ten blocks farther uptown. I think it was symbolic that we touched both black and white worlds that night. That was the way the trip was going to turn out, although I didn't know it then.

Somewhere during the evening my indecision passed. I wanted to make the trip; at the same time I knew that once I undertook the assignment, I would have to do it well, that is, to travel to every representative part of the country. Neither Sions nor anyone else on the *Holiday* staff drew up my itinerary. But I knew I would have to go South. Even as I write this it sounds silly. But I know that it is less silly than it was one year ago; so do a lot of other people now. If I could have done the assignment to my own satisfaction without venturing below the Mason-Dixon line, I would have.

The *Holiday* pieces were to take their own direction. If Sions warned me about one thing, it was the pitfall of over-emphasizing the civil-rights issue. I was prepared to lean over backward to be objective. The civil-rights issue was burning before the public, and being Negro, I attracted the topic as a magnet attracts particles of steel dust. I had had a suspicion that the articles would go that way. I would have been happy if they had not. On the other hand, I am not sorry they went the way they did. People were thinking, it seemed to me; people were concerned; even in the South, where I knew the trip would be rough.

Some subtle pressure was brought to bear upon me not to carry my guns South. It is true that I planned to do some hunting on my trip. But I also fully intended to use them on people *if necessary to defend myself*. The pressure was meant to thwart the occurrence of this possibility. I can understand that. But I fail to comprehend how the people who put me under that pressure could in all good conscience fail to be as concerned with my personal well-being as with their own. If one is willing, one learns every day. I might add that the pressure did not come from *Holiday*.

Does a white American have to orient himself psychologically for some aimless wandering about the country? To a degree, yes, but not a great deal. For me some sort of psychological preparation was necessary. Eventually I became ready, but it was a costly process.

John A. Williams

September 30, 1964

Late in September, 1963, I set out in search of an old dream, one that faded, came back into focus, and faded again. The search was for my America. Some of my boyish concepts of it remained—altered by time and experience. Between these, resting like day-old cornbread, hard and gritty, was what I had learned of America as a black American.

I knew that concepts change day by day, second by second, impulse by impulse, and that 1963, edging past the Cuban crisis of fall, 1962, was a year of change so great that it has yet to be measured. And I felt this far behind the news headlines. I wanted to know how America was picking its way through a transition that was inevitable even though it was being resisted on almost every side.

I learned my America in Syracuse, New York, a city that came into existence because of the great salt beds beneath its foundations. I knew boys named Katzman and Halpern, Carrigan and Finnegan, Popoff and Demetriades, Schalk and Migdal, Storto and Grandinetti. I learned, the way children

11

do, that they were good students or poor, good athletes or awkward ones. I don't know what they were told at home about me or the other colored boys with whom they played tin-can soccer in the schoolyard or football beneath the principal's window. In my own home, on frequent bad days, my parents snarled about "crackers" or "peckerwoods," a vague race of mean people—white, to be sure, but not my friends.

I grew up in a time when the Boy Scouts were still fashionable; I became a Life Scout. In contrast, one of my sons, Greg, dropped out before completing Second Class, and the other, Dennis, never did get full wear from his Cub Scout uniform. Times change and so do concepts. I do not fault them for their lack of interest in the Scouts; rather, I am disturbed that they seem to know so much more about America than I did at their ages. And I am also very glad that they know.

In my boyhood, the Third Reich emphasis on physical fitness had penetrated America, and there were mass demonstrations of Indian-club swinging, work on the horses, rings, parallel bars; recesses were for deep breathing. We saluted the flag, said prayers, and ducked the heavy rulers (donated by the bankers of the city) swung by impatient teachers. Looking up at the summer skies, we never expected a plane to emerge from a bank of clouds—and hardly believed it when it did. The Goodyear blimp, which sent scores into the streets as it passed overhead, was for us the most fantastic creation of our time.

We did not feel in a complete sense that we, the black people of Syracuse, were the victims of any special set of circumstances during the Depression, simply because, there being more white people than black, there had to be, logically, more white people out of work and poor. The fact is that we were poor before the Depression and would be poor after it.

Only when I myself became a teen-ager did the dream of America begin to taste sour in my mouth. I was not a good student, nor was I a bad one. Then followed a teen-age period of being in school for a time and then out of it to help out. I was the firstborn of four. At a time when the white boys I knew were still going to school, I was riding the sanitation-department trucks and tossing up steel barrels filled with ashes. Even some of my black friends had not had to leave school. I spent my evenings dripping bitterness and trying to take extra classes at night to catch up. Because I liked Glenn Miller's music, I started smoking Chesterfields. I started to drink and went through the whole process of seeming drunk when I was not—an obvious attempt to call attention to my plight. But somehow I would be back in time for the football season, the basketball season, the track season; one feels little sense of competition in hauling ashes. And when I returned to classes, my fellow students seemed so young, so out of touch with things as I had known them during my brief sojourns away from learning. I had heard truck drivers and older men discuss their women; I had drunk with them, had sat in joints I had shunned before as "sporting places" (my mother's words). I had sat atop garbage and burning papers and unnamable other objects listening to the other men's rhythms of bitterness, the cadence of despair, the raucousness of desperation. I had seen wild battles among the dump heaps, had seen the flash of knife blades, had walked to a doctor with a man who had a knife in his back. And one morning a man walked between a street sweeper and a wall; the sweeper started, pinned him, crushed him to death. Another morning my partner fell off the truck and it backed over his leg. I came home many times really drunk. I was too young, I thought, to see these things; I had dreams of power, of being a three-letter man. I drank these dreams to death.

By the time the war came, I was exhausted with the fight to keep my original dream of America alive; I was beat to death and war seemed to be a welcome change. My condition by that time was directly related to my color. I could not have made this statement then; it would have killed me. I would have had to reject all that I had.

But the war. First there was the segregated naval base at Great Lakes, Camp Robert Smalls, then the segregated units. I was eighteen when I first crossed the country, going west to the war. I was warm and secure in the bosom of the Super Chief hustling out of Chicago. Like most raw boys of that age, I was fearful that, with the aid of a Japanese bullet, I really would be "going west," as the men of World War I used to say. On the other hand, I had a growing hunch that, since war was a heroic thing, more white men than black would be allowed to die in it. My biggest battles, however, were not against the Japanese, but against the United States Navy and many of my white comrades.

I had more fire then. I raised some little hell. I spent three hitches in the brig, one of them a Marine brig. I was usually charged with breaking some Navy regulation, but I was fighting for my rights as a sailor, black or not. I saw white Marines and black sailors line up for a race riot on Guam. A Chamorro girl told me that she had been warned to stay away from black men because they had tails. My parents wrote asking what was being cut out of my letters. I had endless conferences with the censors and refused to stop writing home and saying that the Navy was rotten. I have a pitted face from the dry shaves I got in the Marine brig. I traveled up and down the islands of the Pacific because black hospital corpsmen were not wanted aboard ship, and I wound up with a land force. A white Texan on a dark night in the New Hebrides was a minute away from shooting me; a white Mississippian who had been there and had dissuaded the Texan told me, "Williams, you ain't like them other niggers." When I told him he was wrong, he laughed. *"You* crazy," he said. "They ain't."

At the end of the war, while the white servicemen were screaming their triumph over the Krauts and the Gooks (in the Pacific the war had been fought along racial lines), I sadly had arrived at the conclusion that America was at still another crisis, but could move to approach the ideal concept of its being or fall far from it. I was hopeful. To live is to hope, but whatever good was in the air right after the war was quickly and expertly snuffed out.

America had become a stranger to my earliest dreams. My early experiences and those in the Navy had had a curious impact: my wariness, or, as some of my white friends put it, my paranoia, grew. But hope, forever ready, was crouched on the starting line. It was there each of the four times I crossed the country, my stomach knotted with nervousness, an eagerness to gain those islands of safety, cities mentioned by railroad porters and waiters and itinerant musicians as being "all right." As I packed to begin my trip in autumn, 1963, I had memories of being refused service in Arizona, of being passed a miserable sandwich through the window of a restaurant in Jefferson City (the window was for Negroes). And I recall now feeling a helpless, suicidal anger when I had to beg for milk for Greg's breakfast when he was four and we were on a trip through Hammond, Indiana; and I remember being shouted at in a crowded Wichita, Kansas, restaurant for having had nerve enough to ask for service.

But there was hope, tensed on the line, ready as always to go. The year 1963 seemed the time, for some reason, perhaps because of John F. Kennedy, whose rhythm sounded right even if the words didn't. With Kennedy the direction seemed right; the old men were out, the young ones in. And the nation was young and becoming younger still.

And in my thirty-eight years so much had happened—so quickly. From dirigibles to rockets; from heavy, lumbering styles in machinery and in life itself, we had come to a lightness, an almost automated, keyed-up way of living. From a depression population we had progressed to one of great leisure. Negroes were no longer being hunted down and lynched except upon occasion, and then the lynchings were not done in the classic manner, with rope and gasoline, with men and women ready to sever genitals for souvenirs. No, things had changed, were changing still. America was stirring as it had never stirred before. It was indeed a time in which to live, and a time to go.

My departure was filled with sun and gaiety, despite the warning of a visiting British writer who moodily declared: "People have a way of disappearing on the road. Why don't you take someone with you?"

I had thought about it, but who? The boys were in school. My favorite dog, Dunhill, a great golden retriever, was dead. My friends were occupied with work. Secretly I was glad there was no one. Conversation can color an observation; an additional presence often can make your actions false: fear turns to bravado; humor comes less naturally, maybe forced into being merely to reestablish the human bond after miles of silence; a good line forged by a view or a conversation goes with the speed of a mountain wind with distraction and is lost to the typewriter forever. Go, then. There was the shopping for camp gear and clothing tough enough to stand long hours of sitting and walking through brush, for drip-dry shirts (an utter failure). Lists of names and places had been compiled. There were the guns to clean once more, for there was the possibility of hunting bird and big game. There were shells to get and the borrowed car to check, since mine was not yet ready. Then, finally, it was time to begin the search.

It was warm that September morning. In New York we

had had four days of surprising cold. The street was empty, for it was Sunday. During the week it is blocked with great trucks and scurrying lifts loading and unloading. There are also the clicking heels of swaying, proud-walking Puerto Rican women garment workers and the hum of sewing machines. After five and on weekends my street is quiet, and the dirty, gray, chipped columns that rise up three floors finally regain their century-old dignity. There is no time like an autumn Sunday morning in New York. It was very early, the sun just over the edge of the East River. The office buildings, which hulk and seem to vibrate during the week, were still and empty. Vistas of uncluttered streets unrolled; traffic lights seemed pompous, winking stop and go with no traffic to follow their directions. Harlem, with nothing to do and no place to go, woke early and commenced its scowl toward the south, toward Manhattan below.

I drove north, of course, and west, for a search begins at the point where the hunter was believed lost. For me, it was Syracuse.

It was for me when I was growing up a city as far removed from New York City as Ogden, Utah. It was my home and I knew it as such: its hills and creeks; its lakes, its alleys, its parks. I knew what the roads felt like after a hot day—soft, so soft you could sink beyond the soles of your shoes in the asphalt; and I knew the winters, when snow came for days on end and rose so high that you had to stand on the porch to see across the street. I remember church picnics and near drownings; scooters made from two-by-fours, roller skates, and crates; and rubber guns triggered with clothes pins; and homes with kitchens as large as the living room I now have. I remember my father playing touch football in the roadway when work was slow, and the slap of the men's leather-enclosed feet as they raced down the street grunting and shouting for a pass: "I'm in the clear, Stosh!" Black men and white men, little men and big men.

What did I lose first? Religion, perhaps, for cleaning the pastor's porch one afternoon I found under a box a number of empty whiskey bottles—a discovery I confided to no one, not even when at a very early age I stopped taking the Methodist communion. As a result, every first Sunday became a crisis between my parents and me, and I had neither the courage nor the words to tell them what I knew. They could drink, but not the preacher.

The second thing I lost in those days when there were still blacksmiths and troughs for the horses was the feeling that I was *just like* Larry Katzman or Hecky Alpert or Vasco Finnegan or Chuckie Sullivan. The awakening came one afternoon while we were reading that children's classic *Little Black Sambo*. I remember the giggles in the class, the swelling that grew in me until I closed my eyes, hoping to open them and find the kinky-headed pickaninny with the great toothy smile gone. When I opened my eyes, he was still there.

That was the day when Larry, Hecky, Vasco, and Chuckie *also* discovered that I was different, not like them, but coal black and with liver lips and nappy hair. And it didn't matter anymore if I could beat them running or fighting or play touch football or soccer better than they.

I saw Hecky Alpert in Syracuse, in a restaurant, and my first impulse was to cry across the room, "Hecky!" but I didn't. I kept watching him, hoping to draw his eye, hoping that a sudden gleam of recognition would come and *he* would cry across the room, "Johnny!" No gleam came, and thus no cry. It was not that he was avoiding me. He no longer knew me. Why was it, then, that I knew him, and surmised that he was no longer called Hecky, but Herb or Herbert? Why had I remembered that his hair was tight and curled, that his teeth were crooked, that he was a whiz in arithmetic, that he fought only when there was no other solution, and that he fought wildly with complete annihilation in mind, as do many meek people?

He had changed and so had Syracuse, a city that had a Negro population before 1769. Italians, Sicilians, Irish, Germans, Poles, and more came to this city on the old Erie Canal. From salt mining and agriculture the city progressed to heavy industry.

It is a Republican city. It was a stop on the Underground Railroad. A small, unobserved plaque on the wall of a downtown building commemorates the rescue of a slave named Jerry from slavery agents. But even cities with vastly more Abolitionist tradition found themselves, during the summer of 1963, besieged with demonstrations. Syracuse was no exception. Having grown up there, I knew how few opportunities there were for Negroes, although people told me I had made the best of them. That the fifteenth ward was a ghetto of the worst kind, and therefore the most corruptible, was well known to its residents and to the police force. I lost any respect I might have had for the law when I was young and saw the police play their numbers free or make mock arrests of the numbers people or take a whore to bed because the night was slow and they knew whores had to agree or face the prospect of seeing a judge the next morning.

But this September Syracuse cops faced something else; the state had come through and trimmed the garbage off the force and the cops themselves had closed the joints, wiped the streets clean of whores and narcotics salesmen. The cops were faced by chanting, marching civil-rights demonstrators who had thrown city hall and other public officials and clergymen into round-the-clock meetings. Everywhere I went the city buzzed with editorializing, gossip, and discussion. And generally, the people who had the most to gain were most noticeably absent from the demonstrations.

"Where are the Negroes?" a newsman demanded of me. "Most of the pickets are white."

They were not only white, mostly, but from the University of Syracuse. A professor I had admired while I was enrolled there had been one of the pickets arrested and jailed. The students were promptly called "outside agitators," a handy phrase used North and South, and designed to obscure the fact that agitators from outside or inside would be nonexistent if there were no problem to draw their ire.

But other things concerned me in Syracuse: my sons, Greg, 16, and Dennis, 13; and another loss of a sort.

I see them and one or two friends rather often, but the changes that were being wrought in the city took me by surprise. I see little of the place except with them and know none of the people who planned the demonstrations, let alone the people who were trying desperately to circumvent them, a move that is national. The pattern seems to be: one, try to get out of it; and two, when you can't, sit down and see what the hell they want.

Greg believed the picketing would help. He seems to me a large boy. He is quiet, demanding through this quietness that attention be paid to him. He remembers when I was there, and he remembers when I wasn't. Superficially, he is a joker. He picks his times for serious conversations because he is basically shy. He will even wait until his brother has gone to bed, although they are very close.

Dennis, on the other hand, is trigger-quick with a quip. Outgoing, he has the kind of unchanneled energy that can make one nervous. Dennis will ride roughshod over you, and if along the way you choose to become his friend, all right; if not, well, all right too. Whereas Greg is tall and tending toward broadness, Dennis is going straight up and has his breadth still to gain. They will attack each other verbally or physically, but will not stand an assault from the outside without one helping the other.

They agreed that the demonstrations would be helpful, but beyond that they did not discuss it, for their heads were filled with notions from books whose essence had very little to do with what was taking place in the streets. Besides which, they have a very special mother and believe, I am rash enough to think sometimes, they also have a special father, despite the divorce. Such a belief, whether true or false, tends to immunize them against outside events; they have yet to learn that true immunization does not exist; mine went when I was younger than Dennis. And yet, at the very core of their beings I have sensed a cynicism so great that I have feared to measure it, and as a result, this time too our conversations meandered.

The trip, however, was a neutral thing. "So how come you're not going to Africa?" they asked with just the right shade of indifference.

"I thought I'd better do this first."

"Alone?"

There it was again. Did being alone mean to them the same thing it had meant to the British writer?

"If it were summer, you could go," I said.

This was a crumb; it wasn't summer. Besides, I have never been sure that their curiosity was as great as mine, especially about traveling.

"Will you send us a card from every city?" Greg asked, his eyes a bit aslant; for this boy every request opens him up more than he likes.

"Yes." I had good intentions when I said it.

"You'll be back when?" he asked flatly, the tone creating quickly a neat wall between us.

"Christmas. We'll spend it together."

He gave a brief, satisfied nod, as if the business of the moment was at an end.

For more than a year now my sons have been talking about going into the service, and I don't really know how to answer them when they ask for advice. They have books on which branch offers the most, how they can finish college before they go in, or how they can do both at the same time. It is all very distasteful to me; I am disgusted with the matter-of-fact way in which they discuss what must be. I take no joy in listening to them, for I recall my own bad days in the Jim Crow service and worry that they too will probably be visited with the same trouble. I suppose it is in the makeup of a father to refuse to believe that his children can be or will be tougher than he was. And so I postponed another discussion of the services until my return.

The last day. The sky was overcast at first, then the rain came, a slow drizzle. I picked the boys up from Sunday school and drove to our favorite cookout spot in the country, where we play croquet and talk when things are right between us and eat hot dogs and drink beer; they snitch mine. Now we didn't talk too much. We sat and listened to the rain springing from the top of the car, watched it bound from the leaves of the trees in the park. "Take care in school," I said—the same foolish thing I say to them over the phone, or every month when I see them. They must get tired of it. Greg's face gets tight at the good-byes, as though he must carry out the role he began when I first arrived. Dennis' becomes more open, more thoughtful.

"Yes," they said.

"Want to tape a message for us?" Dennis asked. Sometimes he lets me play the father.

There wasn't time. "When I call, you can hook it up."

Then it was time to go. I wasn't always used to it. There are times when it seems I have never been used to it. Our world is bigger than what I have described. The important fact is that we have one and move through our paces accordingly.

The following Sunday, a sweep of upstate New York and the Adirondacks behind me, I was on my way to New England. I had prowled through the mountains looking for the lakes in which I used to fish, and had had to return to the southern part of New York. But now I was free again, striking out on another golden day. The thing of freedom to *go* must have been born in me, and I never feel as good as when I am pointing myself away from where I've *been*. But I have noticed that, more often now, I am glad to return.

I stopped for coffee and a sandwich at a diner in Mechanicsville; it was a low building, resting near the bank of the river. There were two females inside. One was old and beefy and had that way of resting her elbows on the bar that told you right away she was the boss. The other was young, not eighteen, and was very new at waiting on tables. The second one waited on me.

"Honey," the older woman said, "ask if he wants cream and sugar too. You gotta ask. Lots of people take it black."

"Cream and sugar," I said to the girl, who was blushing. My coffee was almost gone, but the sandwich hadn't come. When the girl finally came back, a little more at ease than at first, she said, "Will there be anything else?"

"My dear," I said, checking my anger, "I ordered a sandwich too." Her face reddened again; her young eyes went wide and she raised her hand to her mouth. She was afraid of the older woman, and I saw that fear. Her eyes said, "Don't tell on me." I knew that look in Syracuse, that look that so many people have that says, "Don't tell what you must know about me." But she was young and I would want some stranger, black or white, to do for my sons what I was going to do for her. It seemed to me more important than her weakness.

"Sir, I'm *so* sorry," she whispered as she wiped the table.

"Forget it. Just bring me another coffee."

I finished the coffee and tipped her. A fool? An ass? Perhaps, but it was a fine day, and I refused to let a nervous kid spoil it.

Feeling expansive, I took the road to the Saratoga battlefield. Birth pains, I thought, walking over the low green slopes. What would they think now, those American Revolutionaries, of the land they fought for? Fought during September and October almost two hundred years ago, the battle that began on Freeman's Farm threw 9,000 men under Burgoyne (4,000 of them Germans) against 9,000 Americans commanded by Horatio Gates. I walked the battlefields and thought of—what? The German fighting tradition. The Germans: favorite bodyguards of the Caesars. The Germans:

hired out by their barons as soldiers. The Germans: fighters in the French Foreign Legion. The Germans: but for two major tactical errors during World War II, they and not I would probably have been strolling in Saratoga. How lucky we have been so many times when it counted to have good fortune. And it was my good fortune to be free and going to Vermont.

I have never met a person who has been to Vermont and not loved it. It is a state of infinite physical grace. The roads slant upward softly; every curve unfolds a new and exciting vista. It was aptly named; the hills are green and often wounded with daggers of granite and ancient basalt. People do not crawl underfoot.

I first went to Vermont in summer, 1960, to spend two weeks as a scholar at the Bread Loaf Writers' Conference, directed by poet-lecturer-editor John Ciardi. John Engels was one of the many writers I had met there and he liked Vermont so much that he had moved his family from Wisconsin to live there. I was going to spend a few days with John and Gail Engels and their family. They live in Hinesburg, a town so small that you are likely to miss it if you aren't careful.

They live just off the first curve in a red-brick colonial house trimmed with white. A great green lawn and the green flats reaching up into a series of low hills in the distance set off the house.

John and I waste little time on courtesies. So we walked into the living room and watched the Los Angeles Dodgers take the fourth straight game from the New York Yankees to win the World's Series. Some men like each other for their acts, their looks, their intelligence, or a combination of factors. John and I became friends, I think, because we like athletics and played touch football at Bread Loaf. Item piled on item with ease then. He is a poet but doesn't look the way we conceive them; he is six-one and was a lineman at Notre Dame. Like most former athletes, he is always talking about getting back into shape. Teaching and raising a family, together with some professional disappointments, have slowed up his career in writing but not stopped it. I think John Engels is a rare man because he is honest and incapable of deceiving anyone; more than that, he seems to me a man who makes of his religion a philosophy— not the other way around. He is not afraid of life. I think

—although I may be wrong—I was the first Negro he met man to man, intellect to intellect, and he hurt me sometimes, piercing through the anesthesia a black man must build up if he is to survive.

It didn't hurt so much this time, sitting on his front lawn that evening, drinking beer, glancing up at the stars, which always seem so close to the ground in Vermont, and talking about the trip. "Will this be about civil rights?" he asked me. He has a direct and disarming way of asking questions sometimes.

"Whatever's there."

"You've mellowed," he said. "You once said that you didn't think an honest white man existed, and therefore I didn't believe you could see beyond the civil-rights issue."

"I told you that?" I was thinking of his thinning blond hair, blue eyes, and pale skin. I hadn't thought about his features until then.

I probably did tell him, only I'd forgotten. Has any Negro ever confessed that civil rights can be a boring issue —necessary, yes, but boring as well, because it is war and only the sick can ever like war. A man wants and needs peace from travail. If he is not given it, his mind will provide it for him. That is why civil rights can sometimes be as lifeless as a rock. When I told John that, my anger must have been keen. I do not mean to say here that the boredom lasts forever. What I mean is that all the attitudes and arguments, the patterns, the rationalizations, are, for most Negroes, old. I should think that most Americans would get bored with the annual autumn ritual of the opening of the schools in the South.

Perhaps I had mellowed, for the moment, at least.

One of John's friends, who is also on the faculty of St. Michael's College, was Cleveland Williams, a professor of political science. Cleve is a small West Indian Negro (I'm not sure if John Engels was aware of any differences between Cleve and me, however), the father of twins, and the expectant father of triplets. Cleve scoots along with a short, swift stride that matches the way he speaks. Motionless, he seems in motion. A great many Vermonters in the area have become interested in civil rights, and Cleve has been asked to speak at many meetings.

At one such meeting he was asked about the University of Vermont's "Kakewalk," a highlight of the winter festival.

Cleve said the "Kakewalk" was all right, but should be per-
formed without blackface. His remarks were quoted in the
local paper; Cleve says they were misquoted. Letters to the
editor proclaimed "Kakewalk" a Vermont tradition. Controversy grew among the townspeople, among the students.

But as with so many American "traditions," the origins
of the "Kakewalk" have been obscured. Negro slaves, spying
from behind their cabins, saw the grand master's family
going to church or to some other special affair. Since the
slaves knew the family intimately, the majestic airs displayed
on festive occasions were comical and hypocritical. At their
own clandestine affairs the slaves imitated the master and
his family, grossly caricaturing their way of walking, the
twist of the shoulders, the swing of the arms. The slaves
were caught and made to perform, before white audiences,
what the master thought a purely Negro dance. When the
onlookers laughed at the Negroes strutting and swinging,
they were laughing at themselves. Cleve Williams knew all
this, but had the grace not to tell. As a matter of fact, although Cleve and I discussed this at length, we did not
mention it to John, a man with whom I feel most comfortable.

It is a comfort that can only be described as one where
I don't have to pull my punches or keep my guard up.
There are few people, black or white, who give me such a
feeling.

It was a good time to be with the Engels; the weather
climbed into the 80's, the forest floors were gold with billions
of small yellow flowers. We lunched on trout and toast, the
fish right from the freezer, where John had put them after a
summer of fishing, homemade French bread, and cold beer.
Afternoons we walked the hills, saw to the west the Adirondacks and to the east the Green Mountains. I was overwhelmed by a sense of peacefulness. This feeling was shaken
when we returned to the house.

We sat around the kitchen table, John reading the paper
and I watching the way the sun, coming in through the
window, glittered on specks of dust floating in the air. David
climbed in my lap. John was making surly comments about
the news. "Why are you so chocolaty?" David asked. He
pushed firmly against my face and glanced at his hand.
I looked at John, who had already lowered his paper. He
said urgently, "Tell him, John. Now's your chance to explain

that you're a Negro and that there are a lot of different
people in the world. Go ahead. *Go ahead!*" My first thought
was that it was not my job to tell David, but his father's.

Jessica, on her way to the yard, paused and smiled up at
me, as if to give me courage or to apologize for her brother;
she is just five.

I started slowly. "You know Indians?" Only yesterday the
kids next door had asked if I were Chinese or Indian.

"Yes," he said.

John fidgeted nervously, his paper forgotten.

"Well," I said, groping. I wondered, "How *does* one explain oneself?"

"He's different. I mean, he's not white like you, is he,
an Indian?"

But David was scrambling down to go play with the kids
in the yard. "Damn it, John, you flubbed it; you've lost
him," John said, and I had. Perhaps not forever.

I did not buy my maple syrup in Vermont, I bought it in
New Hampshire, where I was beginning to see the hosts of
rusty, joyless New England towns that sat on the curves of
roads, dying, their mills gone South, their only access to
other towns or cities the buses, because the trains too had
left. At one point the sight of each little town, so similar,
so deadening, got to me, and I turned to a French-speaking
station in Montreal.

The smaller cities of northern New England, like the
smaller cities everywhere, I would find, continue to lose
what they so badly need: industry and professionals, such
as doctors. But a transition appears to be in the making;
these areas are adjusting to a vacation economy. Winter
sports and summer living are gaining more favor than ever
precisely because the larger cities are growing larger, and a
few days in the New England countryside make big-city
living more bearable.

Pulling off the road, I headed into a lunchroom that was
surrounded by a motel. A man at a front counter looked
questioningly at me as I came through the door and paused
when I saw no one in the dining room. Bad time of day,
I thought, with no one coming through. That had to be the
reason why it was empty. I moved forward. "Can I help
you?" the man asked. Suddenly it occurred to me that he

thought I was going to ask for a room—and he didn't know how to handle it.

"I'd like a bite to eat," I said, not really stopping, but not moving, either.

Pure, unadulterated, undisguised relief flooded his face. In a fraction of a second he was transformed from a cipher to a really very charming person. "Oh, I *am* sorry," he said. "The lunchroom's closed right now. I guess you missed the sign at the side of the door."

I had. I walked to the car, musing. How much of this would I run into? I had told myself, of course, that there would be a lot of it, a hell of a lot of it, but I believed myself tough enough to take it. Now I wasn't so sure; one never is when one is face to face with it. Yet, it isn't like a war, where every soldier expects someone else to get it. Every Negro expects to be rebuffed, whether he will admit it or not. This does not mean that he *likes* it or will accept it passively. Too many people still make that mistake. A white man, for example, will never know, could never know, what has happened to the Negro to whom he has just delivered an insult. A white man ought to assume that if the Negro before him is twenty-five years old, he has had twenty, if not twenty-five, years of insults and rebuffs, and that that Negro may have had quite enough. A white man ought to assume that, and if he had any sense he would.

After the encounter at the motel lunchroom, I found myself picking out places to stop or, rather, letting them pick me out. It worked like this: you begin to drive more slowly. The eye drifts over this motel or that, seeking some instinctive assurance that you will not have to put your life on the line by asking for a single for the night; that is just about what it amounts to in many places in these United States. Now, there are 29 states that have definite laws prohibiting the turning away of anyone seeking public accommodations. Kentucky had an executive order, but it had expired. Florida and Virginia keepers may not advertise that they discriminate. Louisiana and Tennessee have antibias laws on the books, but they were set down during the Reconstruction period and have not been applicable since. (I have reference to the continental states. Alaska has antibias legislation. In Hawaii state legislation prohibits discrimination only in the payment of wages.)

A law is no law when it is not enforced. In each of

the 29 states in which law forbids discrimination in public places, discrimination in public places exists. There are no exceptions—not in New York, San Francisco, Chicago, Boston. There are none.

I did not find New Englanders crusty, merely reserved and a little curious. I enjoyed a fine fish chowder in Skowhegan, a lusty clam chowder in Bangor. Near Ellsworth, overlooking Union River Bay, I tackled a Maine lobster that, every time I think of it, brings water to my mouth. How can South African lobster tails be as good?

Down along the seacoast I came. The morning sun was glinting brightly off the Atlantic; the fishermen, already putting out to sea, waved to me when I parked and leaned against the wind to watch them.

Boston has never interested me, but I paused long enough to look up some of the Harvard crowd, people I had known in New York City, and a friend with whom I grew up. Bart, the friend, was a thug from his heart and tough. When we played sandlot football, he used to carry a knife behind the pad of his thigh guard. The rest of us were always told not to hang around with him, but of course we did. No one could handle the dice better than Bart or play Tonk, a card game, or get more mileage out of a pinball machine. In those days, if you didn't want the free games, you could have the money. Bart didn't have to be a thug; his folks were well off, but he was a born gambler, a battler. By the time he was in his midteens he had gotten into so much trouble that, in order to avoid further embarrassment to his parents, he left Syracuse and settled in Boston. Now he was heavier and darker and his forehead was covered with the slick scars from street fights. Bart and I leaned across a bar, listening to Lloyd Price and drinking beer.

"You li'l bastard," he said. "How you been?"

As we talked one of his girls came in. "Want some?" he asked.

"Next time," I said.

"For free, man."

"Next time."

"What, are you too good or something?"

"No, but I have to go." She didn't look that good anyway.

"All right. I suppose you want to see where Crispus Attucks died?"

"No."

"Good. Damn fool. Who asked him to stick his black butt into it anyway?"

"Yeah. You going to be home Christmas?"

"What for?"

"Just wondered."

"Naw."

"Okay, I'll see you," I said.

"One for the road, Johnny."

Yes, I thought, and for all the football games in which we used Ossie Solem's 'Y' formation; for all the lead we pilfered from abandoned houses and sold to Mr. Ullman, the junkman. If we found no lead, we climbed his fences, stole bags of rags, and then, the next day, in other bags, sold them right back to him. A drink for all that, Bart, and for the growing up, and one for the road too.

"Yes, Mr. Williams, your new car *is* ready, but you'll have to come to Detroit to pick it up unless you want further delays."

To Detroit! By this time I was ready to go to Vladivostok for that car. I had pictured myself behind the wheel a thousand times. It did not help to know how much the auto lends one status, whether one possesses the status or not. I was ready to give myself over completely to the materialistic life. Detroit, *yes?* On the next plane, overweight and all! How enticing is the prospect of owning that which one has never owned before. Used cars I have had, yes, but a new one, stinking of paint and leather, with the clock and radio working perfectly, a vehicle seemingly with the will of a woman, requiring a nudge here, a touch there, a prayer in this city and a curse in another—never.

There is no other travel like air travel. The waiting rooms are quieter, the passengers more somber, the prayers already begun to give lift to the wings, if needed.

Conversation begins to die as the plane taxis out, and by the time the great metal monster lunges down the strip, dead silence prevails. The ground rips by, the weight of the plane seems too much for the air, and then—miracle of miracles—it is up, bumping its way through the currents of air, its engines throttled, arching over the waters near Idlewild. All this to a fierce assemblage of noise. Quite suddenly the plane seems no match for the unending expanse of sky and cloud. The prayers begin. The stewardesses prance down the aisle, smiles fixed, dresses too perfectly fitted. Coffee, then, or perhaps a meal already prepared, the meat, vegetables, bread, and dessert set in neat piles. Up ahead, in their private cubicle, sits the crew, pressing this button or that, pulling this lever or that, faceless, impersonal. Once in a while the captain tunes in the intercom, announces the weather and the speed and tells you approximately where such and such a landmark is, but you can't see it from 37,000 feet up with clouds racing brutally at the wings and biting at the belly, which seems all too vulnerable. An odor fills the plane. It is slight and if it had color it would be gray. All the Yardley and Givenchy do not conceal it, for it is the odor of fear, the fear of the possible, the fear that comes when one remembers that last week—or was it last month?—that not long ago, one of these monsters came down and there were no survivors. The odor is like that of a locker room, still uncleaned, the morning after the big game. Well, the breaks of the game, but please, someone else's break.

A great, ugly city except for the new structures in Cadillac Square, Detroit sits on Lake Erie within view of Windsor, Canada. It is a city that always looks back to 1943, the year of its big race riot. No city that has had a race riot or a pogrom can forget it. A root goes down and unless dug out, will bear fruit once more. Well and good, but there was the car, a nine-passenger job with over four hundred horses hidden under the new white hood. Red upholstery, whitewalls, automatic. A gas-eater? Perhaps, but comfort and power.

I drove into the heart of the city at almost five o'clock in the afternoon and promptly encountered heavy traffic. Factory workers and office workers and people who had got caught in traffic, lunged homeward, ready to begin the weekend, for which Americans live. They rush snarling from their desks and machines at five P.M. sharp, five days a week, as though released from jail. This is merely an observation; I cannot criticize, for I have been in the office and factory. I checked into a downtown hotel carrying typewriter and bag, rifle and shotgun, a road atlas and *Travelguide*, a listing of places in America where Negroes can stay without being embarrassed, insulted, or worse. I do not believe white travelers have any idea of how much nerve and courage it requires for a Negro to drive coast to coast in America. Nerve, courage, and a great deal of luck.

Again civil rights was the major topic in Detroit.

The "Freedom Now" political party was in the process of being formed of representatives from the Black Muslims, the Group on Advanced Leadership (GOAL), and the Uhuru Movement. Only a couple of days before, pickets staged a demonstration that opposed Detroit as the site for the 1968 Olympics. *IS DETROIT'S SEGREGATED HOUSING READY FOR THE OLYMPICS?* the signs read.

The state legislature had just killed a bill put forth by Governor Romney, and this was taken as a sign that he could not be placed on the national scene as a Republican Presidential candidate. Romney's defeat did not make the big headlines.

My boyhood friend, John Clair, now a sociologist, could tell me what was going on in Detroit, tell me what I could smell but could not see. Scare headlines are not always meant to scare. The most important thing I remember about John Clair—and I remember many things about him—is that once, when we were kids in a Scout camp, he whipped another boy half to death for chopping up a milk snake with an axe. He is now a Community Organizer Supervisor. He is very tall and very dark, and you are surprised to see great, brown eyes, instead of black ones, looking at you. His schools are Atlanta, where he met his wife, Syracuse, and Morris Brown.

Over barbecue and beer, looking at the Friday-night people in line for their take-out orders, we talked. "The Negroes feel that their bloc of votes put Mayor Cavanagh in office. Now they want some benefits. They'll agitate until they get some. White people move to the suburbs to get away from us, but leave the voting power in our hands. They want it both ways: to run and not face the consequences."

What would it be tonight—Leonard Pennario with the Detroit Symphony at Ford Hall, or jazz? Perhaps because of our conversation, neither of us wanted to spend that evening among white people. It was a thing left unsaid, but easily understood. At the Driftwood Lounge, we looked out at table upon table filled with men and women who were black, brown, beige, plum, yellow, and white. There was a looseness there, as there is in almost any Negro nightclub, that you can't find in a white one, American or not. The customers go, in the first place, to really listen to the music. In the second place, a night in a club, while not unusual, is a special thing, for it costs money, which is becoming increasingly harder to come by. In the third place, a night spot is a welcome relief from the burdens of living in a ghetto. On stage, with great flash and soul, was Chuck Jackson, a rock-'n'-roll singer. Opposite him, in a shimmering dress, was Yvonne Fair, who took the magic of the spotlight and made it her own.

We prowled through the Negro section. The night was filled with voices raised in call, of car doors slamming, of people going and coming. In one place—I did not know what it was, there was no music and it was bare, unrelieved in its shabbiness—a young man looked up at Clair. "Hey, ain't you Mr. Clair?" His scowl split and a smile came.

They talked while I stood by feeling awkward, unrelated, and yet, I knew places such as this, knew them so well that they came to have, after a time, a certain charm. I was wondering what had happened to me when Clair finished and led me outside. "I helped him when he got in some trouble," he said. So he felt it too. I had assumed as much right away, but he did not trust that; he had to say it. We had indeed moved far apart, but wouldn't admit it. Once, when we were young, we learned how to trust silences. We had lost that, moved away from that.

In the small hours when we could feel the town slowing up, we sat over beer, and as if to justify our being there at that moment in time, we retraced the past we had shared, passing around the hard parts, laughing at the good parts, revealing triumphs never before revealed, and naturally, admitting no failures.

As he drove me home, out of the ghetto and semighetto, he said, "Man, this town is ready all over again. Guys have been buying guns. Jobs getting tight. Young guys, like the one I talked to, got nothing to do. Any kind of trouble comes as a diversion. And if they can tie that in with striking a blow for freedom, it fits even better."

"There's only one thing to do if it breaks," I said.

"Run like hell," he said. And he had said it.

We found a good eating place, the Cork and Ember, and John, his wife, Lily, and I went there for dinner one night. Neither John nor Lily had eaten there before and it be-

came an adventure. In the hotel I had noticed, when calling
for room service, that there was just the hint of a pause when
the Negro waiters came through the door and saw me. Now,
I am sure they had seen other Negroes in downtown hotels,
but not as often as they see white guests. (Surprise, brethren,
surprise!) Then, that second of hesitation past, the routine
continued as before. I saw myself in the position of the
waiters when, at dinner, I noticed that the maître d'
and the sommelier and the waiters were Negro. There they
were, sharp in tuxedos, crisp in movement, and with just
the barest suggestion of contempt in their demeanor when
they leaned over a white patron and suggested an entree
or a wine. (Do it, brother!)

After we ordered, the chore of selecting a wine was left
up to me. So the maître and I went into an odd kind of
battle. His eyes reflected the feeling that we had no business
there; how dare we. He suggested one kind of wine, but I
insisted on another. He brought still another, and finally,
with a brief glint of approval in his eyes, he brought the
wine of our choice. Perhaps he didn't want us there, in a
place that was frequented only by whites, but he sure knew
we had *been* there. The dinner itself was unexpectedly good:
filet mignon, New York cut sirloin, and filet of beef Welling-
ton. The only other time I tasted Roquefort dressing as
good as the one we were served with the salad was in Louie's
Restaurant in Santa Barbara. If there was one thing wrong
with the dinner, it was the music. I like jazz, and so does
John Clair. But jazz of the upbeat variety, with a group of
musicians clumping all over the stage while you are trying
to eat, never struck me as the right kind of dinner music.
To be sure, we were looked at. We had a very fine table
and our color made us conspicuous. I've always believed
that in many places a Negro does not know the reason white
people glance at him. Perhaps some are thinking, "It's about
time." Others, "Who are they?" And still others, "My God!
Here too!" It is hard to know, for no one tells.

The car was ready now, my powerful white beauty with
the smooth lines, the quiet flash, the concealed power. Cold
air and blue skies greeted me the next morning as I waited
outside the hotel for the car to come. A man who was
also waiting—for what, I did not know—struck up a conversation. At first it had to do with kids, teen-agers. We

saw some skylarking across the street, reluctant to go to
school. He wondered why they were so very destructive
these days, why it was that parents let them get out of hand.
I always listen with half an ear to such talk. It takes more
than physical parental strength to bring up kids; it takes
intelligence and a great deal of luck. In his day, the stranger
continued in a faraway voice, his folks really lit into him
if you showed the slightest inclination to go astray. Yes, I
said, so did mine. The sun was full on the stranger now.
He was slight, and this made him seem to have a youthful
frame, but his face was old and wrinkled. Dirt specks showed
on his nose. When he spoke, he stared intensely at me, as
though pulling agreement out of me.

Kids stole cars or broke their windows, he went on; they
stole when they didn't have to; they were insolent and aimless and always sought the world without wanting to pay
for it.

Where is the car, I wondered.

He had warmed up to his subject. Suddenly he was speaking more easily, more rapidly, and with an accent I couldn't
place. Northern rural? Southern urban?

In his day he had walked miles to school, he said.

Where's the car, damn it, where's the car?

He had eaten tons of fatback and grits.

I looked around for the car.

Suddenly: "What do you think of the Black Muslim
crowd?"

So, white man and black man, getting down to cases.

But now, floating around the corner, the driver languid
behind the wheel, *my* wheel, came the car. *Deus ex machina.*
Just in time. Saved by the bell. So long, bye-bye.

"Do you have time for coffee?" the stranger asked me.

"I have to go." I could see myself over coffee, talking
about the Black Muslims. Maybe I would see the stranger
somewhere else and he would not even look at me. Well,
not today. I'm off.

My sleeping bag was stacked under a seat. My typewriter
rested on the carpeted floor, and my suitcase, packed to
bulging, was squeezed between the seats. I wanted no clothes
on hangers, which would give the people of the South the
impression that I was on a leisurely jaunt through their
region. The California plates that had been put on the car
would do enough to give that impression. In the rear of

the station wagon was a five-gallon can of gas for emergencies.
Left behind at the insistence of friends was the six-millimeter
rifle and the shotgun; they would be sent on to Chicago.

"They're tough on Northern whites going down there," my
friends had said, "even without guns. If they stop you with
them, you've got trouble, licenses or not. They may even
accuse you of transporting arms." I left the guns behind.

Bob Franklin is a municipal judge in Toledo, Ohio. I
met him outside his courtroom. The sun was straight up,
noon. He had me park in another judge's place and we
walked to lunch. I had never met him before, yet there was a
great feeling of ease with him, and not because he too was
Negro. We lunched and talked about a mutual friend, Bob
Johnson, of *Jet.* Franklin was running for re-election, but
didn't look worried.

Like John Clair and John Engels, he concluded that my
sole interest was civil rights. They are forcing me into a
box, I thought while he was telling me about the Negro
population, Urban Renewal, which was displacing it, and
diminishing old line industry, which offered few opportunities for full and steady employment. Urban Renewal, employment, housing and relief rolls apparently were all related
to Negroes and the civil-rights issue.

While he was showing me his small, comfortable courtroom, I asked Judge Franklin how things were "down the
line." He understood perfectly and smiled politely, almost
professionally. "Where do you go from here?"

"Cincinnati."

"You won't have any trouble there. You can stop any
place."

I marveled. When I was last in Cincinnati in 1946, during
the heyday of Bob Taft, a Negro couldn't even move from
the Jim Crow car, which had originated in the South, until
after the train had left the Cincinnati station. Among Negroes, Cincinnati and Columbus, Ohio, were as bad as Deep
South towns, and were to be avoided as much as possible.
"Everything in Ohio is getting to be pretty straight," the
judge said. I looked up at his bench and the flag of the
United States stretched on the wall behind it, and I hoped
this was so.

A few miles outside of Toledo, the speedometer refused
to register. I pulled into a garage and two mechanics looked

at it, one up under the wheel, the other standing outside, the Ohio sun burning his already tanned face and turning the ends of his brown hair to gold. In the end, they sent me to another garage along my route. I drove, trying to match my speed with that of other cars. The land was flat. A thick cover of dust lay upon tree leaves, cornstalks, grass. It was like driving down the center of a dime the land was so level, so uninspiring. In northern Ohio, from east to west, the roads carry you up and down over hillocks like a roller coaster. Not here. Restlessness comes driving in such country, then boredom, and then sleep perhaps. The sun was starting its downward curve and great trucks began to growl away from the loading stations and sideroads, and coughing, crept heavily onto the highway.

The speedometer was fixed and all was ready once more. I had called a hotel in Cincinnati to make a reservation and I was running tardy. I didn't want to run the risk of being late and having accommodations refused me, Judge Franklin's comments notwithstanding. He is an Ohio judge. I am not. I pressed along, for the first time growing a bit tired of the car, of the defensive driving required by anyone on the road, for another's mistake can be just as costly as one's own.

After a good night's rest in Cincinnati, I picked up my first cop on the way to Louisville. I also saw an all-Negro telephone utility and line crew in Kentucky. I have never in my life seen a Negro lineman. When I saw these fellows I nearly ran the car off the road. They waved. I stuck my hand out of the window and said, "G'on, you all." It was said with admiration but the rushing wind took my words and lost them.

The sun was bright and the weather warm. I felt I could have made up a corn-ball song about the Kentucky River that day. I curled around the mountains at a good pace and looked into the deep valleys falling away from the roadside. I had been noticing the bridges. In America, a bridge is generally utilitarian; get it up and get it over. Boom! Boom! There is more art dedicated to the bridges of Europe, a touch of love given to them, an honor paid to the rivers that have been boundaries, escape routes, lovers' gathering places, and inevitably, places of death. The Tiber, the Seine, the Thames, all seem to me to be arched over with wonderful grace. Our greatest bridges, the Golden Gate and the

George Washington, are beautiful, with their powerful masses of steel and concrete spanning vast reaches of water.

Later, passing a turnout, I saw a state trooper's car. I passed it, going with the soft flow of traffic, and forgot about it. I thought I was watching my mirrors with regularity, but when next I looked up, there he was, the trooper, sitting very officially in his car, very sure of himself. All at once I was conscious of the very big, very white, spanking, brand-new station wagon with its California plates winking in the sunlight. He stayed with me for about seven miles. Waiting for an infraction? Radioing and waiting for a reply on HBN 227 California?

He could have passed had he wanted to. Obviously he was waiting for something, waiting to decide what to do. What to do? The South? I was surprised by my own actions. Somewhere I felt that as soon as something of this kind happened, I would panic. Instead, I flagged him down and pulled over myself. He slowed and passed, looking at me very carefully. He stopped ahead of me and came out of his car. He was a tall, lean young man, very handsome with a bluish cast to the areas of his face where he shaved. His uniform looked as though he had put it on just a second before. The wide brim of his hat was as straight as a plumb line. On the front of his heavily creased shirt a nameplate glittered.

"Officer," I said when he came to the car, "I'm having some trouble with a bump in my right front tire." It was true; a bump had developed. "Do you know of a good garage in or near Louisville?"

"Well, let's get to a wider shoulder," he said. He did not look at me.

We drove down the road and stopped again. Together we crouched and looked (rather foolishly, I thought) at the tire, while traffic whistled past. "It's bumpy, huh?" His accent differed from that of the Ohio mechanics; his manner of speaking was crisp, fast. Once he looked at me with his deep-blue eyes, then looked away. "Where you stayin' in Louisville?"

"Sheraton."

He told me of a garage nearby, and then, studying my plates once more, got into his car and drove away. So, if I were a car thief, a murderer, a narcotics peddler, or an FBI Most Wanted, he had the number and the hotel, plus a good description. The trooper no longer had to follow me.

Louisville was a bustling town. The elections were coming up, Louis Nunn against the incumbent, Ned Breathitt. A newsman once described Louisville as a "Midwest city with a Southern exposure." Passing through the lobby of the hotel, the Southern accents began to assail me. Gentlemen sitting in the stuffed chairs smoked cigars and wore wide-brimmed hats. I expected to see a Negro roll out a cart filled with mint juleps. The courtesy at the desk stunned me. I was given rooms overlooking Fourth Street. The bellman came over to pick up my things, an elderly Negro man, very thin and very dry. I let him struggle to the elevator with the bag while I carried the typewriter. When he rang I picked up the bag and handed him the typewriter. "You take this," I said, "and look out for your health."

I could see that old man hauling bags up and down through long corridors, going through the motions of opening drapes and raising windows until someone said, "Here, boy," and gave him his tip. I could think those things and could not stand them; he should have been sitting on a sunny porch watching his great-grandchildren. He reached out with his bony claw and took the bag. "Son," he said with steady cadence, "let's just do this first-class now."

"But——"

The elevator came. I was fuming when I got on. Perhaps he thought I was feeling inferior or something, which was not the case. I didn't want him to drop dead carrying my bag. But all he could think of was doing it "first-class." I was a guest, and he was a bellman. Beyond that, he undoubtedly refused to believe that he was too old to do the work. I trailed behind him down the hall. The bag he slipped along his leg, unsteadily, his breath coming hard. The rooms were superb, old, to be sure, but well appointed, quiet, soothing.

I called the garage after making a couple of appointments and drove over. All the mechanics were white. There was a certain coolness about the personnel. Although the service chief took down every complaint about the car in detail, he was very slow in assigning it to a mechanic. "They'll be through in a minute," he said. But the mechanics weren't knocking themselves out; some, as a matter of fact, weren't even working. They were standing in a group doing nothing: joking, talking, smoking. I walked around the garage and noticed two colored men sitting in a car. One was old, the other was young; they looked as though they'd been waiting for a long time. "Hello," I said to the older man. He nodded. He looked very evil. I walked away.

The mechanics joked among themselves. The service manager avoided looking at me. The time for one of my appointments was growing close. "How about it?" I said. "You've got some men free over there."

"They got a job to do," he said pleasantly. "They'll get to you."

"I'm running short of time."

"Don't worry."

I gave him another fifteen minutes, then climbed into the car and started it.

"Hey!" he said, walking over quickly. "I got somebody for you." He said it with such surprise, as if I should have known that someone would be on the job in a flash. I climbed out and the tires were checked, changed again. Then one of the front-office men came out and drove around the block two or three times with me beside him.

"It's still there," I said accusingly.

"Ah, the tires are outa round."

"All four of them?"

"Sounds like it," he said, squinting to hear the sound better. "Nuthin' we kin do 'bout that. Otherwise, she's fine."

I drove to my appointment and started to learn about Louisville. There was some agitation in the city because of the heat of the campaign into which Louis Nunn had allegedly inserted some racially inflammatory statements. Louisville seemed very concerned with its civil-rights image. Governor Breathitt had already issued an executive order banning discrimination in public places, and a city ordinance was also on the books calling for fines up to $100 if proprietors refused service to Negroes. "Nunn's promised to rescind the executive order if elected," a newsman told me in his office.

I observed that the people seemed determined to make integration work. "Responsible newspapers, papers that have been pressing for this solution for a quarter of a century are partly responsible," the newsman said. "Also, we've been blessed with good mayors, men with some foresight. The presence of a police force trained at the Southern Police Institute, where they are taught to enforce the *law* and not give way to their emotions, has helped."

We both noted that there had been a great influx of white Southerners to the North.

"Bad consciences?"

"That, or perhaps a desire to move where the money is," he said.

Norman Lewis, the newsman and editor of the Louisville *Courier-Journal,* wondered at the prospect of a political civil war since civil rights was the biggest issue before the people at present. The reality of such a war seemed real indeed with Gov. Wallace and Gov. Barnett apparently teaming up, with Southern committee chairmen, blocking the passage of other bills if the administration insisted on pushing through the civil-rights package. Talking rapidly and pushing pencils back and forth on his desk, Lewis went on to say that in Louisville the city ordinance and the governor's executive order (which some people said was unenforceable) came after the fact: the people of Louisville had been mentally ready for integration because certain key people, those connected with the press especially, had decided that it was right.

There was an air in Louisville that seemed to say, "By God, this is going to work!" Yet, they went about it without fanfare. In places of public accommodation I found no hesitation, none of the scanning looks to see if you were the "right kind" of Negro. People looked you right in the eye. And I liked that.

Later I had a telephone conversation with a man I had no chance to see. He was politically close to Louis Nunn. "Nunn's not a bigot," he said.

"Then why has he made those statements? Didn't he mean them?"

"No."

"I can't understand, then, why he would make them."

"Well, Louisville's a bit different than the rest of the state. More cosmopolitan. When you get to the smaller towns and down near the Southern-border areas, you'll find that they think just like white Mississippians. As a matter of fact, there is an unfounded story out that Nunn is supposed to have sent a Negro to the southern part of the state to ask for service—meals and hotel rooms—and when he was refused, he was to have said, 'When Breathitt gets in again all this will be changed.' "

"No proof?"

"No proof. A lot of people still feel that Negroes are not ready as a race, however fast they're growing up. Northerners don't understand the problem, and they're pretty two-faced anyway. Take New England. Why, there are families up there still living off the profits of the slave trade."

I felt too good about Louisville to be depressed by the conversation.

Besides, I had a date. You know how it goes. The fellow from New York gets into town, bringing with him the romance and flair of Harlem, the jumbled intellect people believe still exists in Greenwich Village, the smell of good Scotch whiskey, intimate knowledge of and gossip about the current idols. The New Yorker may be treated cautiously outside his city, but no New Yorker is believed to be without a certain amount of glamour, real or false. He is, no matter what his business, a throwback to the drummer of the last century; he is the salesman who, if he has no goods, has to sell himself.

I did not know my date except that she was a schoolteacher and had been described as a "swinger." Well, all right!

She came to the hotel. I was watching the news on television and I heard the *swish, swish* of soft fabrics and the soft thumps high heels make on carpeted floors. The sounds stopped at my door and the knock came. Good-bye, Huntley-Brinkley; adieu, Walter Cronkite.

I opened the door and she came in. Sometimes I think a man should spend all his time on the road. Yes, there are those times. This was one of them. She had flaming red hair, and she was the color of rich beige. In addition to her hair and skin color, her figure was all that it sounded like coming down the hall, superb, and set off with a black dress (quite short to reveal nice legs) that seemed made just for her.

She had returned to Louisville after living in Cleveland for twelve years. She had been too busy with family and the routine of the classroom to notice the integration of Louisville except when it affected her directly. She had not been out on the town yet, and so, we would share the adventure. Did I detect some nervousness on her part? Perhaps so. If I did, it only made me more determined that the evening would go well. It would never do for both of us to be on edge.

After a couple of drinks, we breezed through the lobby of the Sheraton, through the middle, sensing the turning heads. The Negro porters and bellmen watched us warily, and we passed into the street, walked the few blocks of the warm night to the restaurant. The service—the little courtesies that make dining out a pleasure—left my date numb. When she talked about her friends, I had the impression that they were all stunned by it and were finding it hard to break the patterns they had been forced to live with. It couldn't be true that Louisville was now an open city. It had to be an illusion.

This is what many whites will have to face when the barriers come down. You cannot breed distrust or cruelty or inequity for four centuries and then suddenly expect your victims to be suddenly filled with love, expect them to jump at the new life, which may be (past experience tells us) but another hoax. No, the patience or wisdom American Negroes have so long exhibited will now have to be carried by whites until belief in a new way of life sets in. My date, I think, would be one of those who would not believe for a long time.

How wonderful a dinner can be when the company is pleasant. We had only one bad moment when she said, as if she had won my confidence, "You know what all this has brought on? Colored men and white women. Oh, they've always been ducking and slipping around, but now they've brought it into the open."

It was on the basis of this observation that my date, not from a Negro point of view, but from an entirely feminine one, growing daily in black America, offered her judgment of integration in Louisville: "It won't work." No longer destined to be merely the breadwinner and matriarch as in the past, the Negro woman sees the Negro male edging, however slowly, into the tributaries of the mainstream of American life. Thus she finds herself in competition with women of all races for the man she once considered her very own. She is not altogether happy about this new situation and tends to vocalize her disapproval whenever possible.

On a bright, brisk morning I stood on the steps of my hotel and waited for the car. Louisville passed before me, heavy traffic, awnings going down, crowds gathering in front of the big stores waiting for the doors to open. I watched a bellman load up the car of a couple who had been waiting beside me. Only when they drove away did I look at my own luggage—and find my typewirter missing. The bellman had loaded it by mistake. But mistake or not, it was gone, my weapon, my refuge. How could he have handled it so carelessly? It was like burning a book before it is even written. Or perhaps out of some deep Negro instinct he assumed that the typewriter could not be mine. Maybe the deep instinct went another way; he didn't *want* the typewriter to belong to me.

"We'll get it back," the bellman said to me, easily, without making a move. If I'd been a white man, would his answer, his demeanor have been different? Yes, I think so. Like the girl in the Mechanicsville diner, he was asking me not to tell. B̲ᵗ he had taken what is me, had taken it lightly, and I could see now, without remorse. That typewriter was a part of my life.

I returned to the lobby and reported the loss to the assistant manager. He rushed back to the door with me. Now the bellman's smile was gone. Only during my brief absence had he called the garage and secured the number of the car and the name of the owner. The assistant manager's eyes were cold, his face hard. I could see that he handled these things. The bellman too had his way. He became a younger version of Uncle Tom, Cousin Tom. The assistant manager, placated by the psychological shuffling and hat-tipping, expressed confidence that the machine would be recovered and sent on to New York.

Ominously all directions to Nashville were via the Dixie Highway. Where did it end, the Dixie Highway—in a cotton patch surmounted by a Confederate flag and an *a cappella* choir of White Citizen Council members singing *Dixie?* I thought then of how all travel into the South must dull the hearts of all Americans. If we do not know the South firsthand, we know it through its history, and the reportage from it. We know almost completely the attitudes of its people. We do not have to go there to know that, on the whole, it is not a good place to visit. It is not altogether a sense of fear, but a greater one of shame and of helplessness.

The very roads seemed downhill going out of Louisville.

For the first time I wished the car were smaller and even another color; I wished it were less conspicuous. I picked up the speed signs with alacrity and obeyed them to the letter. I drove slowly through the smaller towns in which, tucked in the alleys off the main streets, manned police cars sat waiting for the unknowing. I felt something close in around me and wished I had not come. This land is death to me, the lovely scenery a mocking set behind which even the crimes of Hitler and his men, if one is to consider the number of people and the psychic damaged involved, grow pale.

Along the roads were tattered open-front shops that displayed quilts and cheap vases, souvenirs of the region, all for sale, all proof that one had indeed been South. Down went the roads, down, then up, sweeping around mountains and great masses of pines stumbling up the hills. There was in the air that morning a certain stillness, a waiting. It is me, I thought; it must be me. Somewhere between Louisville and Nashville, I lost the sense of ownership that I had thought seven generations in this land had brought me. At the moment I did not feel fear, just uneasiness from being acutely aware that I might run into trouble and not be able to emerge without great difficulty.

No man knowingly gives up his life for a reason over which he has no control whatsoever. Yet, heading South, I was placing myself in greater danger than I have ever faced in the North—so far. Now, who is to say that all this means that a Negro would have to die? The Negro—if he knows himself. I have never been tortured, so I do not know how much physical pain I can bear, and I have but a fuzzy idea of how much psychological punishment I can stand. What I am saying is this: I was prepared not to return from the South or anywhere else in America if it were put to me that I was less than a man, less than an American with more here than most, blood, bones, and sweat. I am descended from the one black in every ten who survived the slave raids, the Middle Passage, and slavery. Yes, there are times when I am frightened; I have been frightened and will be frightened again, but I *am* one of the every ten and I have pride enough not to want to disgrace that line.

With this kind of pride, or strength, one has to be prepared to surrender at the flicker of an eye all that life means: children, career, love; Scotch and tight dresses, hunting. This attitude is in direct conflict with the drive of the first of the ten who wanted to live, who was ready and determined to live under any condition. Today the strength of the contemporary Negro is in being ready to die. Together with the loss of the sense of ownership in America, there crept in a sadness, a view of all of it poised to go with the first insult.

Now I used the mirrors relentlessly. And now I toyed with stopping at a gas station, meeting a Southerner on his home ground. Soon enough, I thought, soon enough, and I continued on to Nashville, where traffic was jumping and blazing along its superroads, and poured into the heart of the city. I became lost several times, but pulled into gas stations and shouted, "Hey, where's Buchanan Street?" Invariably the answer would be, *"Buck*anan? Hummm." It was in the Negro section, of course. I drove down the narrow street past the gas stations, liquor, food, and dry-goods stores, and wondered if they were owned by Negroes. Later I learned they were not.

It was very hot and the sight of the swimming pool at the motel cheered me immensely. I swung into the parking lot with a flourish. The drummer from New York was here. At first my reservation was checked at ten dollars a day, but when I questioned it and was questioned in return about my profession, it was lowered. The desk clerk, a young girl, was slow. Even her face was slow. I could see her getting orders from her boss to charge all salesmen ten dollars a day because they made money and were on fantastic expense accounts. In this case, being a writer, I got the cheaper rate for the same room. Ah, Negro business! Perhaps we are not ready.

The temperature was in the 80's and I was eager to get into the pool. Did they have trunks? No. Where could I get some? Down the street at the dry-goods store. The girl's accent was Southern, but altogether different from the accent of white Southerners. What would Shakespeare sound like done with an all-Southern cast, backwoods Southern?

My room faced an open field. On the edge of it stood a hen house. Beyond it was countryside; the motel was at the very edge of that section of town. I drove to the store for trunks. It was filled with the smell of mothballs and goods still stacked in boxes. There were two or three white women trying on house dresses and they all seemed the same: middle-aged, worn, with dull brown hair.

"Mr. Solomon," one of the women said, "he wants a pair of trunks." Mr. Solomon, I thought, are you anti-Negro while Negroes around here are anti-Semitic because of you? Shades of Harlem, Manhattan, New York City. I asked for my size. Mr. Solomon kept his hand on them; they were my size, he said. All right. I just wanted to get into the water. Back at the motel I discovered that the trunks were two sizes too large, but they were elastic and stayed on. But, Mr. Solomon, you knew better. How many other people have you dealt with in such a manner, knowing that the clothes could not be tried on and that, once tried on at home, by a Negro, were not returnable.

I swam until I was tired, then went to my room and slept.

That evening I drove through the Fisk University-Meharry Medical College complex. I was rested and had a date with a very special person. I picked her up and we discussed places to eat; they were few and none of them very special. At the first moment of our meeting I forgot all about the South, but when we sought a place to eat, when she underlined it with, "You must remember where you are," I recalled that I was in the South and how much this can narrow one's life. We found a place that had no liquor license, so that did away with the drinks. But it did have, as if to compensate for what it didn't, a jukebox tuned as loudly as it could go. It vibrated the fried chicken, fried potatoes, and dried peas all the way down.

My friend is pretty much a loner. She is not a Southerner and has faced her time in Nashville with, on the one hand, humor, and on the other with gnawing bitterness at the waste of energies and whole lives thrust into the stupendous race for status among the Negro population. No matter how much individual Negroes may achieve, it counts for nothing in the white community. Around the medical school the visitor hears unfunny jokes about "the Jew," the man the students will have to compete against when they graduate, if they set up offices in the large cities of the North. Already they discuss how to hold their patients, how to keep them from going to Jewish doctors. Little if any of their conversations dealt with being better doctors than the Jews. Their attitude was quite simply anti-Semitic.

Early the next morning I drove to Tennessee State University. En route, I picked up a couple of the students who line Jefferson Street thumbing rides to classes. My passengers were not very talkative. Was this because I was a stranger? I tried to draw them out, but it was such ordinary conversation—classes, football teams, and the like. I quickly shut up. They were not related, but both were tall and dark, their faces immobile, as though in the centuries past, they might have been drawn from the same tribe and sailed across the sea. Moments before I let them out on the big, raw Tennessee State University campus, I was suddenly aware that those kids were unlike any college kids I'd seen anywhere. Just as suddenly I knew why. College was not a lark for them as it was for the kids who went to Fisk. These were burdened with breaking the chain of evolution of their families. Whereas their fathers and their fathers before them were of the soil and were bound to spend their lives in pastoral confinements, these young men were advancing sullenly toward a new world of books filled with ideas, some good, some bad, depending upon the school and the circumstances of its existence. These would leave the land. Even if they remained on it, they would bring to cattle breeding and farming new techniques that would make their lives easier. But most were heading for the new life. I felt this as much as I understood it, for in my family I am but my life and a portion of my mother's removed from the soil.

The kids at Fisk would be an entire generation or maybe even two from the soil. How fortunate to have two generations away from it, and as a consequence, have no guilt for being the first to break from it.

The morning sun was breaking, spewing gold onto the brown dirt reaches of the campus. Here and there were patches of green, but mostly, acres and acres of leached-out soil upon which stood worn Quonset huts. But the important buildings were obvious for their brick, for the walks that surrounded them. And on this campus whose entrance road ended precipitously in rock and dirt, hundreds of dust covered cars were parked. So many cars for a school supported by the state? Yet there they were, only inches apart, leaning at dangerous angles on hillsides, curved around the building. Out of the buildings streamed the students, some, obviously, from the city by their dress, the tight, cuffless trousers, sometimes ankle high, the shirt colors bold, the haircuts neat, studied for the current fashion. These quipped loudly and hiply to one another as they passed from building

to building on grass, wherever they could find it to avoid
getting their Italian shoes dusty. Other males were like my
riders, quiet, almost sullen, and uncaring of styles or dust
as they plodded from one building to another. The girls were
the same, some stylish, some not, but like the male students, the chic ones walked together and the unfashionable
formed on the walks.

"The biggest, most attractive building on the campus will
be the physical education building," I was told, and so it
was. After all, Tennessee State University produced Olympic
track champions Wilma Rudolph and Ralph Boston. Its basketball teams annually clobber the best white teams allowed
to play against its sharpshooters. Its football seasons are generally successful.

The man I was looking for was lifting weights. There
were a couple of uneasy seconds, seconds of study, and then
my mentioning the magic name of the person who suggested
I see the man before me. Now, Earl Clanton, in charge of
public relations, lowered his weights. While I waited for him
to shower and dress, I watched the football managers checking off the equipment. How well football gear fits these
days! Nothing ever fit me well; the hip pads were always
too big, the shoulder pads too awkward, the thigh guards
ill-fitting so that I was often in danger of being castrated.
But with a good fitting suit on, light, pads holstered right,
the feeling is one of invincibility—until you get seven cleats
right in the face. I watched them with a feeling of nostalgia,
remembering how football fields smelled when they were
freshly cut, the odor of franks and hot pop corn wafting over
the fields. . . .

Like someone on a diet of dexedrine, Clanton came rushing out of the dressing room. He set a murderous pace, to
here, to there, to see this person, to see that person, to this
place, to that place. Former athletes seem to run the college
there, coaches and assistant coaches, men whose names and
pictures are legendary to Negro collegiate football. They were
big, hearty men, quick with their big hands, rumbling with
their laughter. Doctors of Physical Education? I did not
know, only guessed. I shared lunch with them; not once
was there a moment of levity. Bantering, mock threats of
violence, pretended interest in me, and once more, the polite
handshakes. Gone.

I wanted to see the chief librarian of Fisk University,

the venerable poet Arna Bontemps. Clanton, being from a rival school, had made other suggestions. I won out. We climbed the steps to the top of the building and found Bontemps gone—to New York. I liked that building which was gray limestone, massive, a Gothic edifice with a clock in the tower. Trees and grass and a stone wall marked the boundary of Fisk, for so long a time a symbol of the "kind of school" to which Negro parents wished to send their children. And in a way, it still is. Just across the street lay Meharry, a school which had to produce fine doctors who were Negro because white schools rarely accepted them as students. Meharry spills downhill beneath groves of trees, walks radiate from building to building.

The college complex: Fisk-Meharry and further up the road and somewhat less in status, Tennessee State. Here, while young people learn careers, they also learn what status *is* and what it *means*. For the male (and this observation need not be confined to Negro schools) a sharp enough girl- friend, one who is able to echo him if he is going into a profession. A car, a sports model, and the more obscure the name of the car, the more status is gained. Clothes in "New York styles" preferably, but if one is a medical student, he need only wear his white jacket to the nearest bar, the white jacket with "Meharry" inscribed on the pocket. This jacket makes up for all the material objects the student may not possess. He is like money in the bank.

For the girl (and this observation also need not be con- fined to Negro schools) a handsome escort, quick with a quip but intelligence to call upon. Clothes, "New York style" or an occasional copy of a little something created in Paris. It helps to have one's own car; it cuts down on the weeding out processes, the rides that automatically include a session of clothes pulling; the girl may not want it, but then, she must be "seen."

But the car is *the* symbol. For many a Negro it may repre- sent some psychic escape. For most Americans, next to the home, it is the breeziest, most glamorous status symbol since the crystal set. And through the streets of the complex, mostly through Jefferson Street, which Clanton called "The African Highway," they gallop, mounted by youngsters with nothing much else to do.

Confederate flags waved mightily in Nashville; they were on radio antennae, they hung from buildings, they were painted on license plates. The biggest one I saw was dangling from the window of a dormitory on the campus of Vanderbilt University. Let me seriously suggest a flag for Dixie. The gray background it could maintain. Upon this imagine chitterlings rampant, a mixture of collard greens, hominy grits and pecans diagonal. In living color.

Clanton and I had spent the one morning driving around the city. The old story of Urban Renewal was repeated here: a Negro slum cleared, new buildings put up, but no Negroes could afford to live in them. "Urban Renewal is Negro Removal." A slogan. I had heard it in many places.

It was afternoon now, and with the drought, the hot weather had continued. Clanton and I headed for the pool at my motel. I came off the taut board, went high into the air, and plunged into the water. For a fraction of a second I moved rapidly through the water and then, *whack!* I came to a dead stop, stars flashing in my head, pain lashing my nose. I had hit the bottom of the pool. I came up.

"What's wrong with your nose, man?" Clanton said. "It's bleeding."

"Hit it on the bottom. Feels like it's broken." But I pushed and pulled it, shoved it up and down. There was no additional pain, but I didn't trust that because there might be shock. I waded to the edge of the pool and pushed it around again. It seemed all right. I had just scraped it.

We went to the motel office. The clerk, a couple of her friends, and a couple of other people who had nothing else to do had been watching from a window. Now they all gathered in the lobby to look at me. "Do you have a Band-Aid?" I asked. The girl shook her head. I had to laugh; nothing in her expression had changed since a couple of days ago. There had been lethargy then, there was lethargy now, to be charitable. There were no Band-Aids and no one made a move to get any. Suppose my nose had been broken and Clanton had not been there with his car and I had not been able to drive mine. Perhaps I would have perished in that goddamn motel, the girl and her friends looking on stupidly.

Thus, we went to the football field where TSU was practicing. The trainer swabbed out the wound and neatly laid a bandage over it. After a while, the pain began to recede. When I called for my friend that night, she stopped and said, "My God, they got to you already!"

John Seigenthaler is the editor of the *Nashville Tennes-seean* and was a special emissary for President Kennedy to Montgomery when that city erupted into racial violence early in 1963. Seigenthaler was beaten rather badly by a mob. He has a round face and quick eyes. A Democrat who was close to the late President, he also saw civil rights as the gravest issue of our time. If it could be solved, the Constitution would have meaning for the first time since it was conceived. "There is now more willingness to accept change where federal government has real influence," he said, "but what lies ahead is the real struggle with old committee chairmen, the Old Guard."

Clanton and I sat drinking cokes. Before us, pausing from time to time to give instructions to his secretary, Seigenthaler sat. The kids on the campuses had made me quite clothes conscious and, looking at Seigenthaler, I decided that he too was "New York sharp" but in a more subtle way.

The Old Guard—men who had won their offices by catering to, courting, and feeding upon prejudice—were on the way out, Seigenthaler said. But I wondered aloud whether young men raised in the same atmosphere of murder in Mississippi, of bombings of Birmingham babies, and the like would not be similar to the Old Guard. Certainly the masses upon which the old men fed showed signs of being far from lifeless. Seigenthaler did not think so. The moves of Wallace of Alabama and Barnett of Mississippi and Faubus of Arkansas had no meaning.

"Within the next five years," Seigenthaler went on, "the Republicans could be expected to make a real drive for civil rights." Was Seigenthaler saying that, if this was to be the case, the Democrats could be roused to more action? Political football again.

He said, "The progress made in civil rights during the past two years ordinarily would have taken ten had it not been for the demonstrations and the demands made by Negroes. We almost had a race riot on our hands Easter, nineteen-sixty-three, but we managed to avert it. Now, that near-disaster makes people think. They don't want it to happen here. They get busy at the same table. They work at getting the lines of communication open. Sometimes we have to do it without the best people because they leave for one reason or another. The Reverend Kelley Miller Smith is an example. He left us to go to Cleveland. Above all, local leadership has to be willing to take the abuse a transition like this brings down upon its head.

"We didn't even look at old Aunt Bessie, who worked for us twenty-five years, for example. And we didn't look at her son who came to pick her up." Clanton and I were standing now, the meeting drawing to a close. "Now, we want to look at Aunt Bessie's grandson—we're beginning to see him, but not clearly, and we can't handle him."

The interview ended and Clanton and I drove back along the "African Highway."

"Aunt Bessie was looking at him, though," Clanton said. "That's how she survived. She knew that family better than they knew themselves. Her lines of communication were *always* open, but their words didn't ring true. They no longer knew how to make them true."

"Clanton," I said, "Aunt Bessie couldn't have had her son alone. A man had to be there."

"Yes, a man had to be there." He was driving swiftly down the street, blowing the horn at pedestrians to get out of the way.

"How'd you like that 'handle Aunt Bessie's grandson' business?" I was shouting now, for the air was rushing into the Triumph sports car as it blazed down the road.

"He meant just that."

"I liked him, but there are holes in his thinking. They scare me."

"They don't scare me."

I am a writer and I am still learning about words, language. There are languages I am sorry I don't know and words in English I wish I knew. But I know enough about my language to know what is being said, sometimes when it isn't. I do not think, for example, that Seigenthaler's lack of reference to a Negro man in his symbolical Aunt Bessie tale was from oversight; rather, I believe, it was from an attitude inherently Southern and white. Until very recently white men have blinded themselves to the presence of Negro males as men. And no matter how sincere white men may be, they will never be able to function as men until they recognize that America is filled with many men who are not white. I am not even concerned with the morality of the situation; morality be damned, for there is morality enough in the true parade of history. The omitted word is as meaningful as the used one. "To handle." The verb has a history of its own that Negroes could write in blood. Picayunish to dissect John Seigenthaler in this fashion? Should I listen to his words alone and not the sound of them? Should I not consider, being a writer, his choice of words?

But then I must also consider the words of Z. Alexander Loobey, an elderly attorney moving toward the end of his time. He had a full, fat face and wore gold-rimmed spectacles. He sat, his belly touching it, behind a desk in his office not far from the capitol building in downtown Nashville. A West Indian who did not seem out of place in Nashville, he had been in the integration business since 1935, when he began with Charles Houston, a man who, had he been white, would have ranked high in the history of constitutional lawyers. Houston also taught Thurgood Marshall, former chief counsel of the NAACP and now a United States judge.

A reflection on Charlie Houston. What waste America produces! He was a man, I am quite sure, known only to Negroes and a few whites.

"Mr. Loobey, are Negroes ready for integration?" We were near the end of our talk. I had heard by now many Negroes saying, because of something done to them by other Negroes, "We just aren't ready." Now, I was asking Loobey.

He paused, his ancient yellow eyes floating up behind his glasses until they were level with mine. "Yes, and no."

"Yes, sir?"

"As a policy, preparation for integration does not exist. Where there is resistance to integration on the part of Negroes, it is often for reasons of self-preservation."

It was noon on Saturday when I left Alexander Loobey. I drove down the "African Highway," past a large liquor store, where, I had noticed, the white men bought only pints, which they stuffed into their back pockets, and Negroes bought fifths. Negroes, with few places to go, usually entertained at home; consequently, they bought the larger bottles. At the motel, workmen, all white, were laying down a new asphalt drive and erecting another wing. This, I thought, showed little faith in Nashville's becoming integrated soon.

I left Nashville for Atlanta on Sunday morning, long before the churches began ringing their bells. Beside me on the seat, wrapped in waxed paper, was a small pile of Southern-fried chicken. The big new car and the bag of chicken didn't mesh. I thought then of a story about Negro soldiers. The soldiers had entrained in the North late at night and had no idea where they were being shipped. Few of them slept, talking and betting that they were going to this place or that. They sat awake waiting for morning and hoping and praying that they were not going South. They knew when daylight came; it came on their left, the east, which meant they were heading for Dixie.

Stories are still current about Negroes who now live in the North returning home in the South; they debate whether or not they should drive their Cadillacs or Lincolns. Some wear chauffeur hats or carry them on the seat beside them; others pretend they are just delivering the car. The stories seem to come less often now, but on the trip I met the daughter of a Midwest Negro district attorney who, when traveling South, will not leave his car for any reason until he is safe in a Negro neighborhood.

Thinking such thoughts, I pulled into Bill and Joyce Eure's driveway. Bill and I grew up together. At one time his family lived upstairs and we lived downstairs. Bill, now a teacher in Atlanta, is very chunky, about five-ten. We used to call him "Dirty Bill" only because he was, in our sports-minded circle, a tough competitor. Pick the sport, Bill Eure starred. And to this day he believes they saved most of us from long periods in jail.

I had visited Atlanta last in 1946, right after the war. And I had gone down early with my cousin and another fellow, named Joe, who lived in Harlem. Joe was a fullback; Moon, my cousin, a guard; and I, a halfback. We went down before school opened to begin practicing football, which all Southern colleges, white and black or integrated, take very seriously. I remember Atlanta and its red dirt; remember returning punts and finding, when the huge ends and tackles were sent down to stop me, how my feet grew wings and so flew past them; remember when no wings came and I ate red Georgia dirt. The day classes began I was on a train heading North. I couldn't take Georgia.

I was most curious about one thing: How could Bill, having been raised in the North, in Syracuse, find a life in the South? Ten days had been enough for me.

"Joe," he said (one of my two boyhood nicknames), "I

don't know. I came down, played ball, got a good job while I was in school, made a little change, finished, got married, and here I am. I don't know."

About three years ago when I saw Bill during a summer visit to Syracuse, he was working on an advanced degree with an eye toward leaving Georgia. But when I saw him for about five minutes early in the summer of 1963, he had changed his mind. "Things are happening in Atlanta," he said, "and I'm going to make it there."

Bill Eure swears by athletics. He coached a high-school championship team in Decatur. He accused other coaches in the area of not trying to make men out of boys, not paying attention to their studies. When Bill moved into the Atlanta school system, he was more or less blacklisted as a coach and has not had a position offered to him since.

Like most of their neighbors, Bill and Joyce live in a moderately expensive house and have two cars. Most of their friends are teachers or professionals. Atlanta Negro society ranks high, and it seemed to me that life there must be largely cannibalistic with the competition for status so keen—status being based on the possession of material objects. The fact that so many people are so well educated cancels out any intellectual achievement. Ph.D.'s are a dime a dozen. Much of this has roots in the theory that, for a Negro to achieve equal opportunity with a white man, he must be better educated. The result is that in Southern towns where there are Negro colleges and high schools, the instructors many times are better educated than their white counterparts. Sometimes, this is not saying too much. Atlanta, with Atlanta University, Morris Brown College, Clark College, Morehouse College (the Negro's Harvard), Spelman College, plus a couple of divinity and undertaking schools, must rate first as the city that produces—and probably keeps —the largest number of educated Negroes of the nation.

Atlanta is the home of "M. L."—Martin Luther King. There was much talk of him—where he lived, how he grew up, how successful he had been. But black Atlantans required a *city* leader; "M. L." was so busy being a national leader that his time for leading at home was always little, and his work, excluding the March on Washington, was not very effective in long-range gains.

Out of the search for a new leader may come Jesse Hill, Jr., editor of a Negro weekly, the Atlanta *Enquirer.* Young

Mr. Hill and I didn't get on too well. At first he seemed to doubt my sincerity; then he indicated that, coming from the North, I was as far removed from the problem as a white man. Subdued heat flashed back and forth. His impatience was obvious. He did say that a summit meeting representing eight organizations was being called to find a new leader for Atlanta. He himself was head of Operation Breadbasket, a well-organized boycott designed to integrate the bakeries of Atlanta and upgrade Negroes already working in them. Milk companies and soft-drink firms were next on the list.

Dr. Albert Davis, a man with a sense of humor (Hill had none) and a vision that surmounts the horizon, could also become a prime candidate. His practice suffers because of his participation in the movement. He is bitter because so few professionals like himself are really and deeply committed to action.

"Atlanta politics are pretty much like politics anywhere," Davis said. "Joining the Old Guard"—Negroes who believe that things are fine as they are—"which acts out a sense of personal belief, mostly, are the Negroes who accept payoffs and who find later, when it's time to make demands, that they can't. And we are hampered by the local courts; we get no breaks there."

Davis leaned back in his chair. A slender man who slides easily between the vernacular of the street Negro and the precise grammar of the medical profession, he went on: "We'll always have problems with 'rabbit crackers'; the backwoods of Georgia are filled with them. They apply a great deal of pressure on city folks."

"But the young guys," Bill, who had accompanied me, said, "are getting tired of paying taxes for two sets of schools. Hell, they have to scuffle just like we do. When those pennies start going, they sit up and look around."

Dr. Davis nodded. "Our big problem is resegregation—the closing up of those places we've already opened. We don't have the followup. The first-class places are usually the ones that open first, but who can afford to take dinner out two or three times a week? They see that we aren't coming back right away and without fanfare reinstitute the old regime. We've got to organize our people so that they will, by turn, keep the pressure on those places, get them used to seeing us in them."

Dr. Davis looked very weary when he stood to go, his

sharp features were somewhat dulled. As if he were speaking to no one he said, pulling on his coat, "Our nonviolent leaders are taking terrible, terrible psychological punishment; the pressure they're under cannot be imagined. They must hold in check the most natural urge of men—violence—when every passing day reveals another reason for the exercise of it."

One of the people I most wanted to meet and talk with in the South was Ralph McGill, publisher of the Atlanta *Constitution* and winner of a number of awards for journalism. I had enjoyed much of his writing and appreciated the importance of the time in which he wrote. It was surprisingly easy to arrange the appointment.

He was not as tall as I had imagined from his pictures, but just as sturdy, just as ruddy. He seemed glad to see me, although he didn't know me. He would be glad, I imagined, to see a Negro walk through the door of his office on an assignment for *Holiday*. In fact, later he implied that. We sat in his office, a room made all the more cozy because of the hundreds of books there. They gave off the smell of pages still to be opened, of slick, freshly printed jackets. Combined with these was the comfortable odor of newspulp from the presses downstairs. My eyes kept sweeping back to the books. The man was inundated with them. I imagined a hundred publicity people in publishing houses checking off McGill's name and saying grimly, "McGill *must* get a copy of this one!"

I found him very deliberate, most cordial, and warm. McGill felt, I discovered as we edged our way into conversation, that no national mood existed, that moods varied from section to section, and that "of all parts of the country, the South is the most complex."

He was leaning back in his chair, his hands folded over his head. Downstairs, on Forsyth Street, a part of the business district of Atlanta, the city hummed on its way. The publisher, now talking about civil rights, was born in eastern Tennessee and had been interested in interracial matters since 1919.

Was there a possibility of a political civil war?

McGill did not think so. Like Seigenthaler, he expressed the hope that change would be more rapid when the Old Guard passed. He stared at the ceiling, and as if receiving an idea from it, said, "We're now in a time of change and examination. It goes slowly. An idea gets going, stops, starts, takes form, becomes alive, becomes real."

Atlanta had changed a lot since my last visit, I observed. He smiled a little. Yes, it had. "New businesses which require trained people, black and white. We need a crash program." He came forward in his chair, its spring catapulting him toward a stack of newspapers. He thumbed through one and ripped out an ad placed by a vocational school that offered courses in Data Processing, Computer Programming, Computer Analysis.

"They'd hire a nigra just as quickly as a white man if he had these courses under his belt. We have a constant influx of rednecks who don't have the training in human existence, let alone formal schooling."

Nigra? I thought.

I had never heard the man on television when he had not said, in reference to black Americans, Negro. Nigra jarred me. His next few words shot past, unheeded. Perhaps he felt comfortable with me, comfortable enough to be himself. I have been told many times that it is easy being with me. If this was the case, then I was being paid a compliment in some subtle way. Further, perhaps for a moment, he forgot that I was black and he was white; that has happened to me also with white Southerners. One such fellow, with whom I was getting on splendidly, said one night during the rainy season on Guadalcanal, "It's raining cats, dogs, and nigger babies." Then he started, remembering that it was me he was talking to. And the start, the jolt, had to include the fact that the man's entire history had crashed about his feet and he saw me as another man and communicated with me in the only manner he knew. When he started, I knew—and he knew—that he'd forgotten to remember that he was white and I was not. The coin has two sides but sometimes it stands on edge. It is a painful and sometimes killing thing to know that. As with McGill, I could see all around, into every corner, and any bitterness, therefore, became impotent with understanding.

Then I asked if he thought that college education had been oversold among Negroes? Negro families were bending all their efforts toward getting their children into college and keeping them there. Negro communities and colleges in the South were being glutted with academicians whose opportunities were being limited by the size of student bodies, by the budgets of the state governments, and by discrimination. Should there not be a return, not to the fundamental Booker T. Washington formulas of working with the hands, of being one with the soil and separate and apart from whites, but of blue-collar work attuned to automation, whose demands were daily growing greater?

"No, college hasn't been oversold," he said. "We'll always need college-educated people." But Dr. Davis, Bill Eure, and others had said emphatically, yes.

And now a wall began to grow between us. He was not aware of it, and it was not a wall as such, but a great difference of opinion. I had been meeting social workers, teachers, college instructors, doctors, nurses, insurance managers, and the like. Only in a barbershop had I met the people of the street, loud with their arguments, unmindful of passers-by, plain, vigorous, kinetic. Between the Negroes of the street and the Negroes of the professions there existed very little contact.

Now he returned to Atlanta and its growth, which he attributed to "local ownership." "Birmingham," on the other hand, he said, "is an absentee-owned town whose owners have no vested interests in the town itself." He talked on, finally giving me the wedge.

To what extent had resegregation hampered desegregation efforts?

In his view, the places that had opened to Negroes (he said this time) were still open to them. And others would follow suit. I wondered what would happen if Dr. Davis and Mr. McGill ever sat down together to compare notes. McGill is white. He doesn't have to go out to dinner when he doesn't want to or can't afford to, just to see if a place will allow him in, merely to keep a foot in the door. I am sure he had reason to be pleased with the changes in the city, changes for which he had been partly responsible.

Was he aware of police harassment against Negroes?

"Rednecks. Country people who are always difficult."

Somehow we got away from Negroes and nigras long enough to talk about the new space installations going up in the South. Would their presence, bringing federal government into the picture as it were, indicate a new prosperity for the South?

He said, "Going back to the national mood—your comments on the space installations remind me—there might be a national mood, one of antagonism, which is building up against moonshots because they're so expensive."

I suppose that when a man is very famous and very good in his field, a great many people beat a path to his door, and in the course of time, there are no new questions he can be asked. All the answers are at his fingertips. I sat there irritated with myself because I could not find within myself that stunning question to ask, a question that would catapult him forward once more, a question that would even explode the warm cordiality in which we sat. The question would not come. We had reached, I felt, a kind of impasse. I liked him very much, but knew him well, instinctively. His parting words, "We are a part of all we've met," told me that in a way he knew me too. He rose, stretched his hands across a pile of books, and said, "Just remember, change. Ten years ago you would not have been here as you are, not even three or two, for *Holiday*."

He saw me, then, as a product of his work.

It was morning. I always started in the morning. Joyce had already driven off to school. Bill Eure stood beside the car, holding the hand of their little boy, Kenny. Last-minute instructions. "Remember, stop for your gas in the large cities, don't mess around with the small places, Joe. As soon as you see a speed zone, *slow up;* don't wait for another sign. Even if you don't see a sign but there are houses, slow down. Some of these places don't post the speed limits until you're on the far side of the town, and by then you've had it. They'll pull you back into town to appear before the judge, but the judge won't be there. They'll tell you that you have to post a bond of fifty, seventy-five, or a hundred dollars, in order to be free to go on your way. If you post the bond, they'll tell you when to come back and appear before the judge. You never come back; who in the hell wants to come back to Georgia? And they *know* that all you want to do is get away. Watch your step, keep your tongue inside your head, and *remember where you are*."

At the last moment, Bill Eure said, "There are three cracker states worse than Georgia: Alabama, Mississippi, and South Carolina." Then he had laughed, as if to say, "Man, I know you're going to be all right." And understanding, I said as I started, "You bastard, you."

A fine goddamn send-off. I clutched my sandwiches and

looked longingly toward the north, but got in the car and drove on south. It was now late in October. The entire South, black and white, was seized with the football madness. It had started in Louisville, then in Nashville, at Tennessee State, talk about the Big Game or how Grambling had crushed such and such a school the week before, 60-0; this was the time of glory for the quarterback, the end, the flankerback, the scatback. Never in my life have I seen so much copy devoted to football, a game I love almost better than food. But too much is too much. It is like the person at the party who, you suddenly realize, is talking too much and is absolutely drunk. For the South, I think football is more than drunkenness. It replaces a pent-up militancy. Securing great athletes by offering full scholarships for many schools has become a full-time job, and the risk of censure by the National Collegiate Athletic Association is well calculated.

I stopped once before I got to Alabama, and while munching a sandwich and sipping coffee from the thermos, I sat and stared at those Georgia pines, so high, neat, and sweeping. I thought to myself: Now I know what the phrase "high as a Georgia pine" *really* means. I finished the sandwich, stoppered the coffee, and continued on my way. There was a lot of road-building going on in Alabama and the signs let you know that they were being built under Governor Wallace's administration, like the signs on the New York City schools let you know that Mayor Wagner was running things. There was one difference: the signs in Alabama had the Confederate flag at the very top. These signs of defiance reminded me of Bill Eure's parting words.

Once I almost missed seeing a red light. I rammed down hard on the brakes and would have hit the windshield had it not been for the safety belt. The squeal of the brakes attracted passers-by of the small town through which I was passing. I cringed in the seat and a youthful dream came flooding back into my mind. After every reported lynching I saw myself in a specially made car, with perhaps Bill Eure and about four other friends, heading South. Built into the front of the car were three machine guns, two .30 caliber and one .50. The two .30's could track 90 degrees to the side. The car, of course, was bulletproof, and being especially built, the engine was supercharged; nothing on the road could catch us.

The light changed and I continued on through Alabama.

Between the border of Georgia and the town of Tuskegee, Alabama, I stopped to pick up five Negro children hiking patiently along the road, tattered notebooks under their arms. I asked the obvious question: "Going to school?"

"Yes, sir," said the boy who seemed to be the leader. His head was long and behind his curled lashes, his big eyes were bold.

"How far do you have to walk?"

"Three mile," he said. The rest of the kids were looking at and feeling the red upholstery, giggling and sneaking long glances at me.

"That's a long way to go," I said. They kept turning, picking out, I supposed, those landmarks that they would not have reached yet had they walked.

I let them out at a narrow path. "Where's the school?"

"It back there," the leader said, pointing. I looked. Far beyond the roadside sat a gray, leaning building. It looked like a disused barn.

"What kind of school is that? Don't you go to a public school?"

The boy shrugged.

"Is that a church school?"

"Yes, sir," he said. "I guess." The others, already running into the woods, shouted, "Thankee, mister." Hurrying to tell about the man with the beard and the big white car with California license plates. Hurry on, then.

I had late breakfast in Tuskegee and then headed for Montgomery, the cradle of the Confederacy. The streets and buildings seemed shabby. There was a listless, to-hell-with-it air about the city. I didn't like it; I don't like it now. I checked in at the only hotel for Negroes. It was a miserable, two-story hovel with restaurant downstairs. The clerk asked me, with some indignation, if I wanted to pay in advance. "Only if you insist," I said.

"Them's the rules," he said.

"I don't think much of them rules," I said, but I paid for the room and left a deposit on the key.

This was the town that started it in 1955, when the Negroes boycotted the buses with M. L. leading. As a direct result, I was told, the attitudes have hardened since then. "Nothing much going on here," an elderly man said. "After all we been through, it looks like it was for nothing. Maybe the buses changed, but not much else. Town's as tight as a drum."

I drove to Alabama State College, which looked, like so many do in the South, like a high school. A group of students gathered around the car. "You from California, mister?"

And I went through the story: "No, I'm from New York, the car just happens to have California plates."

"Where you going when you leave here?"

"Mobile."

"Mobile?"

"Yes."

"Got a gun or *some*thing? They're pretty bad down there in Mobile."

"I got something," I said, thinking of my skinning knife, which was at the bottom of a duffle bag under a seat.

"You better have. They tough down there, mister."

Wouldn't anyone give me a good word along the way, something cheerful?

I looked for a chap whose name had been given to me, but I discovered he had had the good sense to leave. As a substitute, I was offered a professor of sociology. I won't name this man. I am sure that if the Wallace administration wants to give him a medal, he can be found. For myself his name is a four-letter word—and I wish I could think of something worse. I introduced myself, but hardly were the words out of my mouth than he was saying, brusquely overriding me, "Governor Wallace pays my salary; I have nothing to say to you. Excuse me, I have a class to get to."

And he went in his finely cut suit; he went out there to teach young people the mechanics of getting along with one another. I stomped down the stairs, my stomach suddenly kicking up, and took one of the Librium capsules "for the tension." I talked halfheartedly to a couple more people from the seedy campus and crept back to my hovel of a hotel.

I lay in the sinking bed and thought of all those people who had walked all those miles to get a seat anywhere on a bus, and here was a man of position, of some intellect, who in his own quiet way was working just as hard as the segregationists to maintain the status quo. And what was he teaching those kids on Governor Wallace's paycheck? I shudder to think. If equality is to come truly to this nation, people like the professor of sociology are going to have to sacrifice; they are going to have to take risks; they are going to have to face the mirror and see what they are and give up what security they think they have.

There were a lot of hitchhikers in the South. They seemed the same; whether tall or short, they were all thin and made either red or brown by the sun. Some wore battered hats and clutched paper bags in their hands. Invariably they wore chino pants and shirt, and sometimes an old, peaked, double-breasted suit coat. They were all white. It is too dangerous for a Negro to hitchhike in the South.

Sometimes heading down long, dangerously narrow roads, I saw old men or women walking the roadside. They were always Negroes, and a mile or so down the road I would see where they were going: to some general store right out of Erskine Caldwell. At other times, seeing a small clot of men up ahead, I would slow and roll past a road gang composed of one or two white men, the captains, and a dozen or so Negro prisoners. Sometimes the prisoners waved at me and I waved back. I guess they don't wear stripes anymore, and I didn't see any chains, but then again, I didn't look that hard.

I had no trouble in Mobile. I wasn't there long. I passed down Government Street, darted off from time to time to catch glimpses of the Negro section, and returned to it. Without a perceptible change of palm trees I was in Mississippi—Biloxi, Gulfport—and great blue-and-orange signs were bellowing: *K.O. THE KENNEDYS / PHILIPS FOR GOVERNOR.* The land was now flat and sandy sparse, as it is in the Hamptons on Long Island, but the sea was bluer and warm air wafted in, bringing with it the surreptitious smell of salt. Out there were Cuba, Haiti, the Virgin Islands, Puerto Rico. I thought of lazy days in St. Thomas and Puerto Rico, and good swimming, good food, and good drinks. Ah, perhaps New Orleans would be like that, perhaps, perhaps.

I had dreamed long ago of being in New Orleans at Mardi Gras time with my ladylove. Ladylove and I didn't make it at Mardi Gras or any other time. Only now, hurtling through heavy traffic on Broad Street, did I think of the dream and the girl. I smiled as I'm sure she often must have smiled, thinking about it.

From Atlanta I had written to Louis Mason and had made
a reservation at his motel. With the city map on the seat
beside me, I managed to find the way to Mason's Motel on
Melpomene Street. As I curved around the number-two water
pump, gay colors leaped over the gray houses. Mason's Motel!
After the dump in Montgomery the road had to lead up.

Mason was a tall thin man, graying beneath his wide-
brimmed upturned hat. His grin was broad and his eyes
danced. I had the feeling that I had met him before. He
mused awhile and then gave me the M. L. King suite for
half the going rate. But before I could get to it, he took
me to the bar and introduced me to a group of Negro
market specialists, those people who are always going about
convincing businessmen and Madison Avenue how important
the Negro market is, how many millions of dollars it has,
and so on. Since I once had been involved in it, I knew the
types. Bourbon all around. "Drink up, Williams, drink up!" I
drank. They were going to show me a big night. Where was
I from? New York? Yeah? Well, yeah—and veils began to
drop over their eyes. A fresh member of the group showed
up with a new iridescent suit and tried on the coat to cries
of "Man, that's tough!" "It flashes, Billy." The man took off
the coat and launched into what he would be wearing that
night to a dance. The eyes of the others around the table
glittered. These men sold beer, whiskey, soda to the Negro
population, about thirty-seven percent of the total of the city.

They asked me more about myself and the veils dropped
further. Finally urging me to get some rest for the big time
ahead that night, they pressed their addresses and phone
numbers on me. But, as a second thought I wouldn't need
them; they would be around later to pick me up. We'd have a
ball!

I went upstairs to the M. L. King suite and dropped off to
sleep. When I woke it was past the hour for our balling, and
there had been no calls.

"The boys taking you out tonight?" Louis Mason said with
a grin.

"Supposed to," I said.

They never showed. I spent the evening talking with people
in the bar and eating red beans and rice with Louis. One of
his partners came in and we listened to records of Sonny
Rollins, Miles Davis, and Count Basie. We got to talking
about the Mardi Gras, and the partner, a stubby, very friendly

man who would always help carry up bags when the bell-boy wasn't around, said that Negroes ought to boycott it. "They spend a million and half on that thing every year," he said. "But there'll be some who'll go right ahead with their parties and dances, but most of the people I talked to wouldn't, not with Perez down there in Plaquemine acting the fool."

"More money in that damn Mardi Gras than there is in the whole civil-rights movement," a newcomer said, settling at the table with a bourbon and water. "It's a shame what Negroes will do with their money."

The accents of these people were not like the ones I'd heard in Alabama. The speech was colorful: "stomp-down crackers" meaning evil, country whites who'd just as soon kill you as look at you; these were different from the whites who lived in the city itself. "Passé blanc" denotes Creoles who are passing as whites in various schools, stores, and other places closed to Negroes.

I don't know why I thought New Orleans would be different from other cities of the South. My dreams, I guess. I went to my room, got one of the two bottles of champagne that daily came with it (along with beer and soda), took one of the stemmed glasses, and went to the rooftop patio. There I drank champagne and almost fell in love with the city.

A slight breeze blew over the rooftops. I listened to the music and wondered what it was about me that had put the hucksters off. From beyond a row of houses in the next block there came the hustling organ and tambourine sounds of a revival meeting. There seemed to be a lot going on.

The next day I called an acquaintance and made an appointment to meet her family. I also called a restaurant and asked for a reservation for dinner, saying that I was from *Holiday*. The reservation was quickly confirmed, so quickly and effusively that I felt as though the person at the other end of the wire were kissing my hand.

"Wait a minute," I said. "I'm a Negro."

There was a long pause, as if the poor man were trying to catch up with the world and had become breathless doing it.

"Oh, we can arrange to send you some——"

"Forget it."

I went downstairs. It was hot and thunderheads rode the sky darkly. Nothing I had in my bag was cool enough. I drove downtown and got some slacks and a short-sleeved shirt.

Then I went to the old section, the French Quarter. As I was going, I found it difficult to believe that a city as cosmopolitan as New Orleans really was a part of the old order. The appearance of the city, its layout, the people, belie its being as Deep South as it is. I walked the streets of the Quarter and stopped in amazement at the Mammy dummies standing outside many gift shops. They were full-sized, big-bosomed, jet black, and dressed in loud colors. The heads were done up in kerchiefs. Were the white shopkeepers merely making fun of Negro femininity or making light of their own fear of it? The Southern white woman, having been placed on a pedestal, suspects that her man has lain in Negro women's beds more than in her own.

When the Civil War began, there were less than four and a half million Negroes in America, most of them in the South. Of that number, half a million were mulattoes, the result of relationships between white men and black women. Today, it has been conservatively estimated that about 20,000,000 white Americans have at least one ancestor possessing some Negro blood. Inasmuch as blood lines began crossing in the South (and still are), much of the white man's guilt is probably still rankling them. Thus, perhaps, the white male shopkeepers use the dummies to remind themselves (and other white males) of what the Negro female *should* look like—and who then would want to touch her? White females would also be concerned with making the Negro female appear as unattractive as possible. The dummies will stand in front of those shops until the fibers of sex and racism, promoted wholesale by the South and imported by the North, vanish. That will not be soon.

I shopped the Quarter and found only trash, and therefore bought nothing. The clerks hustled, of course, as they do in Greenwich Village; if they didn't have what I wanted, they tried to sell me something else. But there was nothing really worth buying.

I returned to the motel and got directions to the colored restaurant that last night's red beans and rice had come from. There were no facilities for eating in the motel and one had to eat out or bring the food back. I thought I would eat out. "Soul food," Louis said. "Good."

I walked around the corner and got lost. I looked up the street and down, and saw only one restaurant, Nick and Tony's. At the time it didn't even bother me that the name sounded wrong. I crossed the street and went in. The place was rather d?rk. It had a long bar and several men, all white, were standing at it. I walked to the bar, placed my elbow on it, and looked around. The bartender came running toward me. "Outside. I'll take your order from the window." He pointed to the rectangular window. So that, I thought with some vague amusement, was the Nigger Window. That's where you had your food passed to you.

"I only want information," I said.

"All right, let's talk outside," the bartender said. He was a big man, going to pot, with a full head of hair and the kind of face that you forget one second after you've seen it.

We moved outside, and as we did, several of the men at the bar came up behind me and followed us out. I told the bartender, without looking at the others, that I was looking for a colored restaurant. He said he didn't know any and waved in some obscure direction. I left them, never having felt, if indeed I was supposed to, any threat. But the threat was there. Perhaps it was that my mind was on other things, but I just could not, even refused to, cope with the thought of violence snowballing over nothing. But that is the South, and the North and the East and the West. And the moment I entered Nick and Tony's I had committed the unforgivable sin: I had not kept my mind on danger. I had dropped my guard—and had walked away without a lump.

The restaurant that served the soul food was not a place to eat soul food in, and I brought it back to the motel with me. Relating my adventure at Nick and Tony's to the regulars in the bar, I received only quiet smiles; no laughter even. Had I jeopardized the peace and tranquillity of custom, and therefore brought danger to them?

Next door to the restaurant stood an old theater. In the street was a large van that advertised that Gene Ewing, a revivalist, was bringing a "Living Christ to a Dying World." Sometimes I saw elderly Negro women, late for the meeting, rushing through the street, sweat spotting their hastily powdered faces. Ewing was white; his organist was a pretty, dark-haired young woman. Ewing sold Christ and he sold books. My coterie in the bar complained that, if Negroes would give as much to the civil-rights movement as they did to that cracker Ewing, we'd get things done.

When I saw Ewing on the stage of the old movie house, he looked to me as though he could drive one of his two cars across town and join a rock-'n'-roll band without a change of pace. His suits were dark. His hair was cut in the rock-'n'-roll fashion. Perhaps he had hit a gold mine with Negro audiences—he, a white man, preaching to them when they couldn't get into the white churches in their city. And here this man had moved into a Negro neighborhood (at least to conduct the revival) with his giant van with all kinds of leaflets in it, and his organ. . . . ROCK, GENE, ROCK!

I went one night to the restaurant everyone was talking about; I went with one of the men who made the bar his regular stopping place before going home. I ordered fried oysters, and that was the only dish I really appreciated in New Orleans. On the way back to the motel, we were stopped by two policemen. We had been traveling rather fast, but I had assumed that my host knew the risk; therefore I had said nothing. He had a gun in his car, a .32 automatic. The cops found it and began hitching up their pants and puffing their chests preparatory to taking us in. My host got out and took them aside. I sat wondering what a New Orleans jail would be like. My host returned to the car and drove away, the cops following. We went to his place of business, and while I waited and the cops waited, he unlocked the door. A light went on. A couple of minutes passed and my host returned, went directly to the cops, leaned inside the lowered window, then returned.

"How much?" I asked.

"Twenty. Ten each. Gave them twenty-five. They don't make no money. You can generally buy 'em off." He looked at me and grinned. "Scared?"

I thought about it and decided that I had been very scared. I had had visions of people saying, "Gee, the last we heard of John, he was in New Orleans."

One morning I drove out to Metairie, a suburb of New Orleans. I was going out there that night to meet some people, but since I had nothing to do that morning, I thought that I should familiarize myself with the route. I didn't want to be fumbling around a strange Southern city at night with out-of-town plates. I became lost in a park in which I saw only white people. I didn't want them to think that I was trying to integrate it, not by myself. A park guard saw me and asked if he could help. He even smiled. I asked for directions to Metairie Road, and while he gave them to me in a deep

Southern accent, I noticed the nameplate above his badge. It said "Isaac."

Metairie seemed a very substantial community. I wondered (having been set off by the guard's nameplate and having known an Isaac family for many years) if it was one of those strange, isolated Jewish communities of the South; Jewish, but quiet about it; Jewish reformed, and therefore less likely to attract the attention of the indigenous Anglo-Saxon majority. Here, indeed, may have been quiet desperation of the kind the German Jews faced in the 1930's. The South is a spleen-venting land, hating without bound that which it considers different from itself. It hates black and black is the South; there would be no South without it. It hates what is not Baptist or Methodist, rock-hard fundamental religion. It must hate the Jew, and the Jew must feel it, even though the Negro was for a time a buffer. No one who visits a Jewish community in the South can forget it. It is quite like history rushing silently up once again, and although all eyes see it, or at least feel the force of its passage, no one can or will do anything about it. There are single individuals who see the larger picture, who see history looping around the same old corner, and they go out from their temples after they hear the words of the Torah and get beaten and sometimes killed.

I went back out to Metairie that night and met a group of people, many from Tulane University. I was the only Negro present, and although I was with friends—I felt that very much—whenever I heard one of the men or women speaking, with the accent, a certain wariness came over me. It was as though I could see all around them while only looking at the front of them. We did not talk about integration, except in passing, as it affected Tulane. We did, however—and I found this strange, even though I became quite caught up in it myself—talk at great length about South Africa and its apartheid. At the end of the evening, I took my leave and drove back to the motel, noticing as I got closer and closer to that particular colored neighborhood how heavily patrolled it was. I had noticed it in Nashville, in Atlanta, and now here. Well, I'm used to it; I come from New York and the police do quite a patrol job in Harlem.

At the motel I packed, got another bottle of champagne, and went to the patio. My last night. The place reverberated with Lloyd Price singing *Misty* to a really socking beat. And from across the rooftops came the sounds of Gene Ewing leading his horde in a romping, stomping, organ-banging, tambourine-clattering finale. I went downstairs to say my good-byes to the bartender, who whipped out his own specially mixed Martinis. There were two white men sitting at a table. Detectives, my mind flashed; they had that look about them, that sure, loud way of laughing, the way they sat. And more important was the way the bartender kept feeding them drinks with his two-faced smile: one of them, empty of all but shape, and one for me to see that he was putting them on with buddy-buddy. Lloyd Price boomed on. I stood with my back to the detectives and the bartender fed me two of his Martinis.

I went to my room. As I undressed, my eye fell on the pile of newspapers I had collected. The top paper, the New Orleans *Times-Picayune,* carried a three-column photo of three Dallas policemen subduing a picket against the hood of a car. In the background other pickets are milling around, carrying signs that read: *HOUSE THAT HISS BUILT* and *WHO KILLED BANG-JENSEN.* The head over the photo read: *POLICE SUBDUE OVERENTHUSIASTIC STEVENSON CRITIC.* That paper was for Friday morning, October 25, 1963.

Jackson, Mississippi. That name, on my mind when I awoke next morning, depressed me. When I came to New Orleans four days before and people asked where I was next headed, I said lightly, "Jackson." But, as the time for me to go approached, I muttered the name of the city, and people, sensing what I felt from the way I had said it, merely nodded and said nothing. Jackson. How much nicer to take a plane to Puerto Rico and forget about Jackson. Who was I kidding? Hell, I didn't want to go to Jackson. Then, turning over in M. L.'s bed, I remembered that I had already come through a part of Mississippi, driving along carefully, looking at the sea and palm trees. Yes, I said to myself, you've been to Mississippi. Besides, think of all those colored people who've always lived there. That's *their* problem, I thought in the shower.

Jackson is my mother's birthplace, and was her home for a time. I was born there. My parents were married and made their home in Syracuse, where I was conceived (I refuse to give all my heritage to Mississippi), but they returned to

Jackson for the birth of their first child, according to the custom of that time. Thus, in my family, a line of "free" Negroes on my father's side, and one of former "slave" Negroes on my mother's side, were merged.

Some years ago, my boys asked me, "Dad, where do we come from?" Although years before I had started thinking what to tell them, I was startled. Quickly I mentioned Jackson, but I was in panic. A man *ought* to be able to tell his children where they come from. I envied those Italians who return to Italy to visit their homes, the Polish and Hungarian Jews who return to see their relatives, the Irish who make the hop to Shannon and go off in search of old homes and friends. But the boys and I, seeking our lineage before Mississippi, moved to the map of Africa on the wall. We looked at the West African coast, and with falling voices and embarrassed eyes concluded that we could have come from anywhere along the 3,000-mile coast and up to 1,500 miles inland. Then to books with photographs of Africans. Did we resemble any of the people shown? Around the eyes? The cheekbones? The mouth? Which were our brothers? Another check: which peoples were brought to Mississippi? Ah, how can you tell, when they arrived in coffles from other states, already mixed with a hundred different peoples? Mandingo? No, most certainly not. Kru? What, then—Baule?

"Dad, where do we come from?" Up to great-grandfather, some trace; beyond him, fog. We came out of fog. We did not perish in it. We are here.

But Jackson lay north; that fact offered some consolation, for I had tired of watching my step, had tired of creeping along five or ten miles below the speed limit while white drivers tore along at twenty or thirty miles above it. I had tired of down-home Southern cooking, soul food. Let them sing about it; now I know the dark, greasy gravy, the greens cooked to a softness the consistency of wet tissue paper, the grits, the red-eye gravy, the thick, starchy rice. But I ate breakfast, one of soul food, and then I took a Dexedrine tablet. I drove out past Metairie to the Pontchartrain Causeway. The twenty-four-mile drive over the soft, blue waters was hypnotizing; it was as if the only fitting climax to the ride over that stretch of steel, concrete, and asphalt had to be a plunge into the lake. At first, up ahead, there was only the suggestion of land, a silvery haze rimmed in a darkness; only that and the causeway with one or two cars on it, going

and coming. The land at the northern end of the lake became solid, took on color, green and brown. Then the lake
lay behind me, clean, small, dancing morning waves simper-
ing now for other drivers. All I could think was that I was
now in "stomp-down cracker" land, and I had to start watching my step all over again. I began searching for pecan-
stand signs. I had seen many en route to New Orleans, thinking that I would pick up a bag or two later and give them
to Ola, my mother. "Here you go, baby, pecans from down
home." Something like that. But there were no more pecan
stands.

I stopped for gas and again the ritual of the South was
trotted out; a Negro attendant came to take care of me. The
white attendants, in the stations that can afford this silly
double standard, take care of white customers. Before long I
had threaded my way across the border and back into Mississippi and a couple of names assailed me: Emmett Till,
whose murderers wrote an article, got paid for it, were
acquitted, and live still; Medgar Evers, of course; and all the
other nameless ones. The land along the way was flat. Although I watched the speedometer and the mirrors, sometimes the car seemed to have a mind of its own. It would
leap forward like a new colt, and it would be seconds before I could get that big, fat motor to simmer down, be-
have itself, and keep me out of jail. "I'm gonna let you
run, baby," I promised it. "Later."

My *Travelguide* had given me the name of a hotel in
Jackson, and I came upon the city cautiously, looking for
the street. From the south, the city sweeps from a plain to
a modest hill, but the overall aspect is one of flatness and of
rigidly dull buildings. The pace of the people was easy, one
of assurance. I saw small groups of Negroes sitting together,
as if for moral support. Used-car lots filled the street on
the east and small hardware stores to the west. Driving up
the sweep of the low hill, the stores improved in quality and
in merchandise. Following directions, I drove off the main
street, went two blocks, and suddenly the streets were filled
with Negroes. I had arrived in the Negro section; it seemed
boxed in. Almost at once I saw two colored cops; they were
the result of summer demonstrations, and seemed, in their
new uniforms, as proud as kids in new drum-corps suits.

The hotel was very much like the one in Montgomery,
even to the key deposit. But why run a place like that sim-

ply because Negroes, having no other place to go, have to
go there? Segregation has made many of us lazy but also
has made many of us rich without trying. No competition;
therefore, take it or leave it—and you have to take it. The
slovenly restaurant keeper, the uncaring hotel man, the
parasites of segregation have only to provide the superficial
utensils of their business. I had coffee in the dingy little
dining room and rushed out, overwhelmed by the place,
which did not dismiss the code of Mississippi but enforced
it to the hilt.

I fled to Jackson State College, where an old friend was
teaching and coaching. He was in a class, but came into
the hall and brought me before his class; I think he was
teaching first aid. I say "I think" because I could not believe that whatever it was could be considered a course for
a college.

"This is my old friend, Johnny Williams," he said, tower-
ing over me. "He's a writer. You basketball players—we
played ball in the Navy. John was a guard. Good with the
hands. Two-handed set." That dated the hell out of me. No
one shoots with two hands anymore. "Say something, John."
That was my introduction to Jackson State.

Somewhere this must end, I thought, walking around the
campus later. Tennessee State, Alabama State, Jackson State,
a pattern. High school-like buildings, surplus prefab buildings, some grass, some dirt. Here, you colored people, take
this! But was I seeing these campuses through brainwashed
eyes perhaps? I have seen many rolling among soft hills or
edging up the sides of valleys, overhung with chestnut and
maple and cedar. I have seen domes and columns, baroque
and Gothic, cushioned lecture seats and marble walls inscribed with gold; I was spoiled.

I wrestled with these thoughts and finally knew them to
be, however brainwashed I was, true. No great ideas of the
past stalked these bricked halls or sandy stretches of walks.
When the state legislatures of the South created the Southern Negro school, they thought they knew what they were
doing. Books, and teachers, and space. Build what you will.
But the white schools had grass, and baroque and
Gothic structures, and great ideas sometimes trod those halls,
unminded.

But out of the wastelands whites and Negroes together call
colleges, there has come, for America at least, the rebirth of

the greatest idea: that a man is a man, is free under sky and over earth. From brick buildings so new that they still sparkle red, from dingy prefabs with reused floors, from out of the desert, and despite many of their teachers—from here have come sit-ins, freedom walks, kneel-ins.

Since my friend was a coach, he was called "Coach." Since his friends on the faculty were also coaches, he called them "Coach." Thus it went at lunch. I was introduced to some people in the English Department and looked forward that afternoon to sitting down with them, but I never did. My friend said that maybe they didn't want the meeting because it would reveal their lacks. The magic words had been: New York and writer. Later I thought that they may not have liked my friend and therefore would not be bothered with me. People who dabble in intellect often have an abhorrence for athletes or former athletes. Oh, well, one if by land, two if by sea.

More than half the day was gone, and my friend showed a curious disinclination to talk about the obvious. I had honored his attitude at first, then felt that it would begin leaking out. But it didn't and I asked him why, like Bill Eure, being raised in the North, he could live in the South, in Mississippi, which is the worst of the South.

With a heavy sigh that indicated that he knew he would have to answer that question, he began. "After the war I went to Kentucky State. I've been in the South a long time now. We have this house. I have my doctorate. I make good money and I'm in a position to manuever for more. I've got security, Johnny," and he reached over and pushed my knee. "Up there—you know how we lived in my town—we had nothing and couldn't *do* anything, couldn't go places. It was a big thing when we came to Syracuse to play you guys, and if we couldn't stay overnight, we'd bitch like hell. Here, I keep my nose clean. I don't look at white women. I have my contacts. Hell, everyone in this business has his contacts, better have 'em. I've our own doctors for the athletes. My wife works, not hard. She has an easy life and would rather work than stay home. She has her car, I have mine. Johnny, I ask you, what in hell would I have had up there?"

Security. You are damned if you have it, and *god*damned if you don't. Big house, two cars, a yard, television, a savings account. Good, good, but at what expense? Oh, this is not true only of my friend, it is true of most Americans who almost invariably confuse security with status. And they saddle themselves throughout brief lifetimes with jobs and bosses they don't like, associating with people they detest or even hate, just for security and/or status. My friend was looking at me for some kind of confirmation.

I nodded, too depressed to go on, too confused by the disastrophism of time. In the early life of my parents, it was the Southern Negro migrating to the North who gave that section life, but my friend was an example of the reverse: for a cloistered but secure kind of life, he had come South. I remembered once when we were playing ball, my friend had punched a white boy from Texas who was on our team. Duff was the boy's name. I remember him because every time he looked at the basket, he scored. My friend had hit the white boy because he had said "nigger," hit him so hard that Duff had dented a locker when he was slammed into it. Duff hadn't meant anything by it; it was just his way of talking, like Ralph McGill slipping into "nigra." "Remember Duff?" I asked.

"Yeah," he said, "I remember Duff."

I suppose all the way down I had noticed that the elite among the Negroes, the academicians, the professionals, and the like, were as estranged from the masses of Negroes as the whites. If New Orleans is any example, the people I knew there were not of the campus, not of the professions, and they seemed totally without leadership. Where, they seemed to ask, do we turn for it? At least they talked about the movement. In Mississippi, few did.

What can instructors so far removed from life give their students?

"We give them a cycle of ignorance," a Jackson man said bitterly. "The college instructors have created a cycle of ignorance. Many instructors are ill prepared to teach, and the only reason they do is that in the South the legislatures don't care how well or little prepared they are as long as they make the shoddy mark set up for them. They in turn pass on a haphazard education to the students, many of whom become teachers themselves. From the 1962 class, for example, seventy-six students became teachers; only eight went on to graduate or professional schools; five went into service; two became secretaries; five are unemployed, etc. Seventy-six teachers. They will pass on to their students what their instructors passed on to them, and so down the line. Yes, they go to the big schools in the North for advanced degrees, but not because they're really interested in the courses. More money."

The man who was speaking was not a teacher. Strictly speaking, he was not even a professional. His occupation (mortician) has been a necessary one ever since people began to die. A part of his bitterness may have extended from the fact that he was not a part of the academic circle, that the title, preceded by a comma after his name, was a screaming joke. But like my friend, he too had pecan trees in his yard and two cars in the driveway, a station wagon and a Jaguar; I saw these through a great picture window.

It is never bad that one wants to make money. But there are those professions we believe to be ones of dedication rather than profit. Teaching is one. Yes, it is true that even though profit may be the first consideration, some of what the teacher learns during those hot summers in the North may filter down to his students. But if the motive isn't pure, can the method be?

I knew there were students in Jackson who were very much involved in the protest demonstrations and voter registrations, but they wore no badges, and no one pointed them out. I knew one co-ed by reputation, but was given very little help in locating her.

On the way to Tougaloo, where my mother, Ola, went to school, my friend said, "Johnny, I don't want you looking at these white girls. Even with those sunglasses on. Not even out of the corner of your eyes because, if the man stops us, I'm going to tell him you're a stranger, and I'm just giving you a lift." It was supposed to be funny, and I guess we did laugh out of a sense of embarrassment. He, embarrassed because he was telling me the truth, even though he was laughing, and I, because I was ashamed for him. Even as we were sifting through the dregs of our laughter and the reasons for it, we pulled into a gas station. It was a poor one, for a white man waited on us. When my friend handed over his credit card and signed, the attendant said, "You the first left-handed colored man I ever did see."

My friend said, laughing again, "See there, I brought you luck, didn't I?"

Infinitely more beautiful than Jackson State, Tougaloo

Southern Christian College was set among grass-covered mounds, within touch of a half-timbered land, and a forest in the background. I tried to picture Ola walking through the iron grill-worked fence when she was a youngster. When she went, it was a domestic school where young Negro girls were taught that their mission was to serve white people, unless they could find something else, by accident, and the chances then were rare. Ola has spent better than half her life in other people's kitchens and bedrooms and bathrooms. Like the mythical Aunt Bessie, she knows more about white people than they can ever know about her. I hoped the campus had been as nice then as it was at the moment.

Although, at the moment, the place was buzzing quietly. White men had been riding past the campus at night and firing blindly into it. Co-eds had become unsettled, and male students now mounted night guard. My mother would call people like the raiders, "night riders," and every Negro who has ever lived in outlying sections knows precisely what it means. A woman or a girl caught alone at night was automatically subject to mass rape. A lone Negro male walking home, subject to a beating. It was for these reasons that my grandfather, who had five daughters to worry about, kept a loaded rifle slung above the door. He knew how to use it. The trouble with these male students at Tougaloo, however, was that they shot at everything that moved, including, sometimes, instructors returning from Jackson. Perhaps they knew what they were doing.

Tougaloo reminded me of a kibbutz in Israel, isolated from the cities, always within range of the enemy, and yet carrying on the daily routine as if the threat of sudden violence did not exist.

I met the Reverend Edward King, chaplain of the college and civil-rights leader. A slight, pale, brown-haired man, he was rushing to Hattiesburg to bail out some of his campaign workers. King was running for Lieutenant Governor, on an independent ticket with Aaron Henry. This was the first mixed ticket in Mississippi since Reconstruction.

It was my final night in Jackson. An eerie kind of darkness was falling, partly because the weather was suddenly turning cold. I felt disassociated; I had not found the family roots there, no distant relatives, no one who remembered my grandfather, Joseph Jones, or his family. What had I expected? I remembered how, one by one, my relatives came North, the aunts and uncles, and how each one turned to help those remaining in Mississippi to get out. Over the years we heard of cousins who had moved up to Chicago or Washington or Pittsburgh. There was nothing there for me. Now our roots scrape along the concrete walks of cities, trying to get down into solid earth once more.

I went with my friend that night to a practice session of his basketball team. His players were all fast and lean, all on full scholarships. He put them through their paces, the lay-ups, the feeds, foul shouts, two-on-ones, three-on-twos.

"How they lookin', Johnny?" he'd call out.

"Great," I'd reply.

I watched him. He was getting gray and fleshy in the face and full in the gut, and I knew that he would never have been head coach of a college basketball team in the North. Never, never. Then I realized that in the middle of a hate-filled land he had found what he wanted: the thud of swift feet on a hardwood floor, the acrid odor of sweat, the challenge of competition, and security for his family. I drove back to my hotel. When I checked out the next morning, the boarders in the dining room were talking about oil drilling going on and hoping some would be discovered on property they had. They would be rich because, as one said, guffawing into his coffee, "All the scared niggers done left Mississippi and ain't got no more claim on anything." More laughter, general this time, in time to my exit.

There are two reasons why Greenville, Mississippi, is unlike Jackson. One, it is on the river, and thus for decades has been vulnerable to ideas and people from outside the state. Two, the Hodding Carter family lives there and publishes the *Delta-Democrat Times*, a "liberal" newspaper. I had talked to Hodding Carter, Sr., in New Orleans, where he held a chair at Tulane. Failing eyesight had forced him to turn the paper over to his son, Hodding Carter, Jr. I had driven northwest, through and around the low hills, through Vicksburg. I thought, as I drove carefully through the neat, quiet streets of Greenville, This is a place where a man ought to be able to relax. But still I was very cautious when I asked for directions to the paper, and I usually got some vague reply and wave. "Down that way." I should have been more relaxed; I could have been, I think, for I had been in the South long enough to know that whites and blacks weren't continually at each other's throats; that their back-yards touched and that they sometimes borrowed tools from each other and chatted across the back fences; that they shopped in the same places, depending upon neighborhood. I know, because in Atlanta, in Nashville, in Jackson, I heard cashiers say "Thank you" to Negro customers, had seen clerks waiting on Negroes go off to the storeroom for items that were not on the shelves. There was not the cleared space, the No Man's Land, the demilitarized zone. No, lives dove-tailed.

I waited for Carter. He hadn't come in yet. I sat on a bench and stared at the police station across the street. Next to it was a high mound, covered with grass. A levee? ("Tote dat barge, lift dat bale.") Like the next scene in a film there appeared, in front of the bleak view of jail and levee, two young men. One held a briefcase. Carter, I guessed. He kept turning to look at me as the conversation ran on briefly. The other young man passed out of view; the police station again was on camera. Then the other young man, swinging the briefcase, entered the office.

"Mr. Williams?" he said, pausing before me.

"Mr. Carter?"

"Yes."

"Yes."

He excused himself, then asked me to follow him into what might be called the city room. It was rather small, but there were a great many desks and phones. Carter was handed a proof. "Excuse me." When he finished, there were orders to give, and then we went into his office, a dark, leathern kind of place, comfortable, with the kind of air that would make you unburden your deepest secrets with a glass or two of white lightning or Mississippi corn. It was a world away from the bright, battered, cream-colored city room; there was something solid here, I felt.

In the dimness—the office faced west—Carter seemed to have light hair. Strangers, like medieval knights challenging one another on a narrow path, must also have their preliminaries, the chance to study, to plumb, to prepare the reserves for loosing or retire them altogether. I knew something about the Carters—not much, to be sure, but something. I knew that even though he was away from home, someone was guarding his family with a loaded firearm. I knew that he had learned to live with threats on his life and on his family's with a minimum of nervousness. This was the price, not for crusading, but for holding and advocating a view unpopular in the city as well as the state—namely, that a law existed, a federal law, and should be obeyed. The Carters were not for Negroes but for law, and because they were, in the minds of the white masses they were "nigger-lovers."

Of all the newspaper people I had talked to, only Carter said, "It's going to get worse before it gets better."

The other newsmen must have been aware of the steady approach of widespread violence, but they avoided the problem as if to wish it away. Carter: "We almost had a breakthrough here last summer. The Negroes demonstrated, the police didn't hamper them. It wasn't like Jackson. Then it went; how or when or why, I don't know. It was washed away."

For Carter there was not even the hope that with the changing of the Old Guard the situation would be altered. The throb of violence was too near; only a miracle could avert it.

It had become almost a macabre game by now, asking questions and having them answered, or making comments and having them enlarged upon or whittled down. And I found myself trying to concentrate on what he was saying, to find some new nuance. No, civil rights had us as slaves on the waterwheel; we had to go around and around. The questions we asked, the answers we gave, bounded from one corner of a closed box to another, like Mexican jumping beans. I tried to conceal a sudden, billowing tiredness, but Carter saw it. "What's the matter?"

"Tired," I admitted, not at all surprised that I would admit it to this stranger, who, in a larger way, was not a stranger at all. "Tense," I said.

"I'll bet the hell you are," he said and grinned. "First time South?"

"Since nineteen-forty-six, but I was born in Hinds County." His nod was an understanding one.

As we parted he gave me directions through a less troublesome part of the state to the border. But driving away, I knew I had to take the other route, the one where trouble lay, in order to live with myself and in order to overcome the shame I suddenly felt to confess my tiredness, my tension, to this white man. Drive the cliff edge.

The land was flat, the earth powdery. Trees rimmed the distance, so far from the fields that I could not tell what they were. Cotton fields, Negroes pulling long gunnysacks, and I thought of Ola and her sisters and brothers, and wondered what it had been like for them to pad between the bushes snatching off the cotton, dumping it into the bag in one motion, for speed meant money, money meant survival. There were fields filled with peas and corn. How even the land was, empty almost, as if even the great Mississippi had fled in terror, leaving no trace, not even an immediate valley through which it had once coursed.

Above, the sky held blue. It was colder now, but the drought continued. I edged through the dangerous towns, tired but somehow hyperalert, seeing what wasn't always there and hearing what was without sound. The twin pipes of the car stuttered out behind me. North. Cleveland. Clarksdale. Ah, there was a town Carter had warned me about, but I was through it and on the open road again. Tunica, Hollywood, and the land continued flat, but the timber was growing taller. Now the fields began to tilt upwards, the timber thickening, the brown, powdered earth gobbled up by grass. Eudora off to the right, and then, right on the Mississippi-Tennessee border, Walls! Coffee now, a ham sandwich, and a rest. The next town was White Haven, Tennessee.

I picked up a Negro Marine near Memphis. I saw him up ahead, shot past, eyeing him (he was doing the same to me: "All right, you bastard, don't stop"), and then stopped. As soon as my taillights flashed on, he came running. He was a cocky young man, proud of the corps, proud of being the only Negro in his platoon. I was glad to drop him off. After a phone call, I edged around Memphis, darted into West Memphis, Arkansas, to visit a friend briefly, and got back on the road. I wanted to make southern Illinois before I stopped. More coffee and sandwiches lay beside me. Through western Tennessee, threading my way through mountains in the falling night. They turned from green to gray and from blue to black. The night became my ally, hiding me from the police in the small towns. I know many Negroes who travel in the South only at night. I was not so conspicuous now.

Now I knew how fugitives felt when they crossed those borders, waiting joyously for starlight.

The drone of the car was making me sleepy and I lowered the rear window. Cold air came snapping into the car, whipped at my ears, numbed my nose. I should stop now, I told myself, for I was driving with my left foot on the gas; my right knee had almost locked on me and I had it stretched out toward the right-side door. There was no place along my route where I could stop in safety. And the rule among Negroes who travel in the South is: don't sleep in your car. I had now reached the stage where the headlights of oncoming cars and the lights of towns blinded me for a second, and I knew that soon I'd have to stop. Where was I? Tennessee, Tennessee, Kentucky! Kentucky, Kentucky, Illinois. Finally, Illinois. Let it have changed in this section, let it have changed.

It had. After fourteen hours, I was in a warm room and a warm bed, after hot food and a bath to soak my knee.

The next morning, a few miles south of Paxton, the cars that were coming toward me flashed their headlights. What was wrong? Was something falling off the car? Was the tire split and the tube showing through? I drove on, up the Illinois plain. Then I knew why the drivers had been blinking at me. Up ahead, I saw a state trooper standing beside his parked car. He stepped in front of it and pointed twice at me, his mouth forming the words, "You. You." Speeding, he said. Had I known the driver's code of that region, I might have been saved from a speeding ticket. I sat in the car smiling while the ticket was made out. Those drivers in the hurtling cars didn't know me; they only knew, having passed the waiting trooper, that I was in trouble. Strangers passing in the first light of a cold Illinois morning, they had extended a hand and rushed on. They had done their part to help me circumvent the law, if indeed I had broken it. Strangers can, sometimes, unite, if only for a moment.

I arrived in Chicago about noon, scuttling along the Dan Ryan Expressway or, as the natives call it, the Dyin' Ryan or the Damn Ryan, because of the high accident rate. I was remembering the March morning twenty years ago when I left the train, found my way to the Great Lakes elevated, and wondered how anyone could find his way in a city so vast, so enveloped in the smoke from the mills of Gary. It seemed so long ago. Still driving into town, I was remembering the imitation whiskey during the war, the jitneys hustling up and down South Parkway, Lindy-hopping at the Parkway Ballroom and the Pershing; and remembering my great-aunt, who used to sit up and wait for me to come in from Liberty and try to hustle me off to church if the next day were Sunday; remembering Tiny Bradshaw and Charlie Parker at the Savoy, the boxing ring next door, the smell of fried chicken and fish that permeated 47th Street; remembering Marlboros when they had celluloid tips, red and ivory; remembering girls and one New Year's Eve on Calumet Avenue when people were opening windows and shooting into the street with pistols; remembering Chicago hippies in wide-brimmed hats, draped coats, wildly pegged trousers, and knobbed shoes; remembering hitching a ride with a young ensign one morning and how we crashed into another car and crawled out unhurt.

Chicago had changed since then. New buildings hugged Lake Michigan. The Southside extended thirty to forty blocks more; 63rd Street was no longer the boundary of the Negro community. I once had a girl in that neighborhood, and she would not let me visit her if I had to walk the streets alone. Lake Meadows and Prairie Shores now rise and view the lake; the ghettoes, here at least, were gone.

Bob Johnson is managing editor of *Jet* magazine, a Negro news weekly. He is a very small man, dark, electric, demanding of himself, his family, and his staff. I had known him since 1949, when we met at Syracuse University. Now, at lunch with Bob and Hoyt Fuller, editor of *Negro Digest,* a tall, sharp-faced unruffled man, I felt myself loosening, laughing at everything, enjoying my Martinis, emerging from mild shock. The dark fears of the South were behind me. The thought of the legislated anarchy that exists down there, and of my only answer to it, which was to slap it down if it slapped at you, slid to repose in the back of my mind.

There were times when I did not love Chicago at all—1946, 1953—but now, like an old love you've never forgotten, it insisted itself on me. Of course I knew that much of it had to do with the sense of freedom I felt after the restrictions at every turn in the South. Even an illusion can be infinitely more satisfying than the stark reality of nothing at all.

There were breakfasts in restaurants overlooking Lake Michigan, dinners in quiet places, and aimless rides to nowhere but the heart of the senses. There were parties and late hours and more dinners in exotic places with exciting foods. And women. How wonderful Chicago was with them, all sizes and colors and shapes. It was like New York, a potpourri, an invigorating blend, stylish, chic, with the rhythm a big city forces you to adopt. In Chicago the drummer from New York had nothing to sell. New York, isn't that a little place somewhere in the East?

A day or so before the Army-Air Force football game I went to the *Jet* offices in a building near 18th Street, a building quiet and tasteful, with old wood and green carpets, photomurals and good-looking secretaries. Bob and I had been talking when all of a sudden a flurry began in the outer office. Joining the people at the window, we saw a great red, white, and blue bus. "Cassius Clay," the inscription read on it, "Liston will go in eight."

"That goddamn Cassius," Bob said, laughing.

We moved away from the window, and I was thinking of all the people who had crossed the *Jet* threshold besides Cassius Clay. I could have spent a whole day sitting in the lobby and watching the idols come and go.

One of my personal idols lives in Chicago, Dr. E. E. Hasbrouck. When I was young and in the Navy, he made that big raw city seem less so. Doc went to Syracuse University after kicking around the town, hustling enough money to get through high school. He finished and went on to medical school, but was asked to leave by the med-school director, who arranged for him to finish at Howard, which Doc did. He hurdled the professional barriers, but he suffered the personal anguishes only Peter De Vries' Wanderhope could absorb and still seem happy, maintain a thriving practice, and raise a son. Late at night, when quiet finally came after our hours-long chats and drinks and records, I wondered whether he slept well or not. I found myself being solicitous at times over morning coffee, and then felt foolish about it. If his tragedies had been mine, he probably would have said, "You'll make it, hoss, just hang on in there."

I had just started to feel human again. Actually, it did not take long—a day or two at the most and I was able to file the South on a shelf. The white people I met in Chicago, and there were not many, I met without rancor, without any ill will. Yet, there had been times in the South when my mind in its desperate cage had envisioned for me a life of no contact with whites. Stupid, but the idea held me together, and it was an idea not of hate but of survival. Chicago changed that. It was a blessed, tipsy island over which a great amount of intelligence spewed. Just as I was at the zenith of normality, I went on a local radio show. It was called the Hot-Line, and from all I had heard, it was a good show.

My interviewer talked mostly about writing and civil rights. The line was lighting up. One man asked, "How does I get this book I done wrote published?"

A lady said that a friend of the family, a young man, was interested in writing and that he was a very sweet and sensitive fellow.

And then, *the* call.

"Mr. Williams?" He had a young, white-boy voice.

"Yes."

"Have you ever been to Africa, Mr. Williams?"

"No."

"Then why don't you go?"

Loud laughter, fading, and then the click of the phone being hung up as I was saying, heatedly and automatically, "Because the average Negro in America has six or seven generations here, probably more than you, and has more right——"

"He's gone," my interviewer said, "he's gone."

Did I still believe that?

I thought about it the entire next day while I was preparing to leave Chicago. Could I have given that boy a better answer? Damn, it irritated me.

But now I had to concern myself with the car. I had left it in a garage for a complete check, and to make sure I got it back on time, I had tipped the service manager ten dollars. It made all the difference in the world. I wonder why Americans find serving other people so demeaning? In many places in the world whole populations subsist by serving tourists, for example. Perhaps there is a conflict in our culture that makes service generally so sullen, so filled with contempt.

The car was ready and so was I. I loaded from Doc's house, locking the doors after every trip, as cautioned by Doc. "Once," he said, "I had my car down there, near the house. I'd forgotten something, so I had come back upstairs.

Went back down, and damned if the thing would start. Lifted the hood and the battery was gone. Five minutes. Lock the doors between each load. They'll take those guns first thing and *may* use 'em on *you*." The guns had been sent ahead but I had picked them up my first day in Chicago. I said good-bye to Doc, eased out of the driveway, and was off again.

Forty miles north of Chicago, I slowed going through Downey, Illinois, the station where you got on or off for Great Lakes. I had driven Greg out here once when we visited Chicago, and he posed in front of the guard shack, head hanging a little low, the guard checking some sheet or other on his clipboard.

And then Waukegan. I never think of that town without thinking of Jim Crow, Great Lakes style. When my class graduated from the Hospital Corps School, most of the men were sent to the Marines directly or to other hospitals. About four or five of us remained at the Lakes, but they didn't know where to billet us; they were not about to integrate us into the white barracks. They gave us a remodeled garage with private showers and telephones. We met several girls from Waukegan in the hospital chow hall; they came in to work every day and went home at night. We each got a girl, and before long they no longer had to take the slow train ride to Waukegan every night; they simply drifted up to the garage, showered, settled down. Communal living. We were sorry when our numbers became too large to continue living in the garage. We had to give up the girls because there were now enough Negroes to fill the whole downstairs of a barracks. I brushed Waukegan, laughing.

It felt good to be on the open road once again. I found the drivers in Chicago most selfish, but they were behind me now, scrambling through the Loop, zipping around Lake Shore Drive, killing one another on the Dan Ryan Expressway. I let the car out and it jumped ahead, moving cleanly and easily, and the joy of having so much power at toe tip filled me completely. Here it was, the ground-level height of Everyman's automated existence. Open the doors, press a button and lower the window, turn the key, set the gear and mash down. Beneath the hood, currents surged like flashes of lightning, and hundreds of horses snorted, kicked, and began to gallop. Two and a half tons of brightly burnished metal, resting on rubber hoofs, bucked for one second, then soared ahead.

There had been times in the South when I hated to leave the car because it formed a vault of safety. But in New England and when I was emerging from the South, I did not want to get out of the car because of the sense of power it gave me; power to move rapidly, for miles, at so little cost of energy to myself.

On the road, there are always those fellows who, poking along, see you coming and decide, I'm not going to let that fellow pass *me!* And they begin zipping it up, and when you finally pass them, they turn and deliver the venomous stare. The old animal competitiveness, I guess, but since I've never been like that in cars, I'm at a loss to understand it. Nor do I understand country folk who drive out to the intersections of the main highways, poise there as if waiting for you to pass, but then, with studied slowness and a wide turn, pull out onto the road while you stand screaming on the brake pedal.

As I had the feeling of going downhill en route to the South, so I now had the feeling of going uphill through northern Illinois, Wisconsin, and Minnesota. The Illinois plain was but a memory now; the roads wound through hills and mountains, through thick coniferous forests, past dead and dying little towns with sturdily built homes, some a century old; and there were glimmering lakes and rivers and duck floating in close to the shore. Occasionally, spearing up, catching the sunlight, was a pheasant, his flight swift, beautiful, short, vanishing on the opposite side of the road.

Stopping in various places in these states, I was either ignored or paid too much attention to, and I don't know which disturbed me the most. I think I prefer anonymity. In Duluth, a city that climbs the side of a hill and overlooks Lake Superior with its ore-laden freighters easing in and out of the harbor, I had dinner out one night. The restaurant, the Flame, sits on the lake's edge. I sat alone at the table, clear across the room from the bandstand, but noticed that the leader of the group, who doubled on violin and trumpet, kept staring across the room at me. He spoke to the rest of the musicians, and from time to time they all looked my way. I wanted so much to shout across to them: "It's all right fellows, I'm not a musician, and I'm not really concerned that your music is lousy—a jazz violin always is."

But then I'm always being mistaken for a musician. Perhaps it is my beard and color. Invariably in some night spot, no matter the city, a musician comes over and says, "Hey, I know you, good to see you again. I'm sorry, what's your name again?" Along with this go hearty handshakes and backslapping until I tell them my name. "Piano, you blow the piano?" (There is a very fine pianist composer named Johnny Williams.)

"No."

"Trumpet?"

"No."

"No. What do you blow then?"

"A typewriter."

I think the musicians in the Flame were relieved when I left. They were, all things considered, pretty bad, even for Duluth.

There is not much to do in the cities and towns of the northern plains. Night comes with a thudding finality, and the restaurants and bars are usually quiet places where a man can reflect on his day, or escape reflection on anything. The Russians are the big bad boys out there. One headline spoke of Mr. Khrushchev with the informality of the New York *Daily News: NIKITA WARNS OF MORE CONVOY CRISES.* After the success of TV team reporting, à la Huntley-Brinkley, I suppose it was natural that this style would become the vogue, especially with NBC-TV affiliates. But, to use the tandem announcers to report city budgets and traffic accidents and anticipated thousands doing Christmas shopping seemed to me ludicrous and pretentious. However, there it was. You could tell the stations that had money, for they ran film on their news shows; the poorer ones used stills and narration.

I had passed places where snow had fallen, but none came down while I trekked the northern plains. There was rain. For days the sky was overcast. Sometimes rain came down, sometimes it didn't, but always threatened to. Mornings were never pleasant now and the driving itself became monotonous, with flat, black earth spread all around and only a dun-colored hillock to break the monotony from time to time. My beautiful new car was spattered with mud and dirt; its value was now purely utilitarian, for there was no sun to show off its beauty. Except for the cars on the road and the occasional town and one passenger train I saw rounding a great curve outside Duluth, the earth seemed uninhabited. I took a side road and it was worse. By the time I arrived on the outskirts of Grand Forks, North Dakota, I was mentally beat and needed something to lift my spirits.

It was in 1960 that I had heard some ugly stories about Grand Forks, the kind of stories that were so commonplace in America during World War II that after a while they stopped being news at all. I wanted to see the town and talk to some Air Force people at the nearby Strategic Air Command base. The town itself was small, misshapen, and gray; it sat upon the plain apologetically. Most of the buildings and homes appeared to be made of wood. I checked into one of those motels that still pay tribute to the old West. There was a corral, hitching posts, and of course the bunkhouse. I lunched quickly, got directions to the air base, and got behind the horses once more.

At the gate of the SAC base, the guard looked at my authorization very carefully. He was from Virginia, his duty plate showed, and had a heavy accent. When he called the Public Information Officer, I believe he wanted to say, "There's a colored fella out here." But he looked at me once —I was standing close to the phone—and made the call straight.

When I walked into the PIO office, a sergeant asked me to wait because the lieutenant was out. A Negro airman, second class, sat at a desk across the room, trying to stifle a smile. He winked a couple of times. I made a note to talk to him. I had heard that prejudice and discrimination in Grand Forks were not at all unlike some Southern cities. I wanted to know what it was like for a Negro airman to live there. I wanted to know, for my sons lean toward the Air Force and because I am concerned about this world being blown up by some madman. I am concerned whether that nut is black or white. I wouldn't be at all happy to know that a Negro, enraged by prejudice, crazed by discrimination, decided to take his hurts out on everyone, but we are well within the realm of that possibility.

Suddenly everyone in the office found things to do after the sergeant gave me a copy of the base paper, the *Peace Garden Trident*.

"Where you from?" the Negro asked me.

"New York."

"Manhattan?"

"Yes."

"I'm from Brooklyn." He smiled and winked once more. Surely he had something to tell me.

"Where you staying?"

"Motel about eighteen miles back toward town."

"I know that one. How long you going to be around?"

"Until tomorrow."

"Like wrinkled steaks?"

"Wrinkled what?"

"Chitlins."

"Chitlins? In North Dakota? Yes."

"My wife and I are having them for dinner. Come on over."

There was the nice thing I wanted to happen.

When the Information Officer, a tall young man with a slightly pitted face and undistinguished brown hair, came in, he was dogged by a reporter from the Minneapolis *Tribune*. There had been a brawl in town involving some airmen. One of the airmen was critically injured and in the hospital. Were the airmen Negro? After some anxious moments, I learned they were not. I was relieved. While the lieutenant and I talked, I was conscious of the Negro airman smiling his secret smile. Did no one else see it? When the officer's room was clear of the reporter, we went in. At first I tried to discuss the routine things such as "offensive posture," how long it took to get the bombers off (15 minutes), the establishment of Minuteman Intercontinental Ballistic Missile sites on the base, the Hound Dog, which the bombers carried.

"Since the emphasis on being ready to go is just as important as living normally, there must be some mental conflict among the crewmen. How many——"

"The crews are watched every minute on their four-day alert," the lieutenant assured me.

"How many psychiatric cases do you have in, say, a year?"

"Don't know offhand, but those people don't get up. Every man in the crew watches the other men. Each one is carefully and routinely checked out."

"You had a severe housing and racial problem here a couple of years ago. How's it go now?"

Without pausing he said, "We have three hundred new

base houses. They take care of seventeen hundred family units. We don't have any racial problems here. The town's wide open. Our boys get along all right."

We'll see, I thought while he was issuing a pass and assigning the young Negro airman to take me around. We went downstairs and got into my car. He drove. As we went down the road he turned to me and smiled. "You shook 'em up in there."

"How do you mean?"

"The sergeant didn't know what to do with you. That's why he gave you a copy of the paper. I'm one of the editors. And the lieutenant didn't know what to make of it all. When the call came in that there was a guy out there from *Holiday,* we expected—you know, a white guy. Then you came in—" He started to laugh.

The airman was in his early twenties, a nice-looking kid. He went on, "I don't know why the lieutenant sent you out with me. He wasn't using his head, you shook him up so much. There's a lot going on here."

"Like what?"

"It's a bitch here!" We passed through gate after gate, pausing to show the pass to the guards. "I'll let you talk to some of the guys. Don't use my name though, I'm getting out in January. After that, I just don't give a damn, but they might take it out on my friends who still have time to pull."

We cruised down the flight line and I stared at the silver birds squatting there. I interrupted the airman's bored monologue describing the planes, their capabilities, to ask, "Where's the lieutenant from with that accent?"

"Michigan, but the whole damned place is filled with accents, mostly from the South. Crackers all over the joint."

We arrived at the Guidance Control Center, a cement and steel building, rather like a vault, a mortuary, with most of the space given over to banks of computers, long, dark, formidable-looking objects. A staff sergeant explained the functions of the computers, but I could not fully absorb all the things these machines could do. Nor could I really comprehend why the planes were out on the line, heavy winged with fuel, the Hound Dogs nestled in their armpits. The readiness of it all stunned me. SAC says in some of its material: "If a SAC bomber or missile is ever launched in anger towards an enemy . . . SAC will have failed to carry out its objective of preserving the peace." To be ready for ready for war is to be ready for war, and all the fine slogans do not obscure that fact. But, strangely, I had the feeling, seeing airmen striding up and down the walks, that they believed the slogans.

When the sergeant in computing turned me loose, my head swimming, the airman from the PIO office led me outside. It had been gray all day with spotty rain in the morning; it had stopped about noon. Now, it was coming down again as we stood, getting wet. With my guide was another Negro. He didn't wait for introductions. He said, "Can you help us?"

The Control Center framed his leaning, slender figure. Behind me was the flight line and I thought to myself, No, not twenty years later, *still*. But I fenced, I fished for my illusion. "What is it?"

He saw through that stupid question and did not embarrass me. Because it was raining, I thought suddenly of Greg and Dennis; it had been raining when I said good-bye to them. Can I help? What could I say? What could I do, no matter how exciting the prospects of tackling the entire Force? The second airman flushed livid. He was dark, and now his skin took on an ugly, purple color. He began ticking off on his fingers: "We get the lousiest houses in town. We can only be served in two or three restaurants. Our officers, mostly from the South, don't back us up; they don't even care."

"What about the Negro officers?" I asked. The sergeant who had shown me the computing systems passed and the airmen waited until he was out of earshot.

"Nearly all of them are on the crews and they stick to themselves as if it couldn't touch them. Once in a while some cracker gets drunk and calls them 'niggers' in the officers' club; everybody laughs for a week."

My guide spoke now: "We get the stiffest sentences, bar none, for minor infractions. And don't let something happen with the cops in town. They'd forget all about us out here. The white guys really get upset when we have dances and some of the colored guys bring white girls from Winnipeg. We've had one or two rumbles already. They hush those up right quick. There are no colored women here, except the wives and daughters of the personnel. The single guys go all the way to Winnipeg when they have time off rather than hang around this dog-ass, Jim Crow town."

"Your congressman?" I asked.

The second airman was also from New York and lived in

Adam Clayton Powell's district. He turned his face up to the wetting skies in disgust and shifted his feet. "We wrote to Powell and he checked around; some brass told him it wasn't so, and that was that." He spread his legs and placed his hand on his hips. "Look, you can use my name, that's how much I don't give a damn anymore."

I felt fatherly when I said, "No, you don't want to do that." But I knew the feeling. God, how I knew the feeling, the feeling so many young Negroes now have. Let the body become the object of opposition; let them move it; let them take your life, if they will, but get there, all of you, mind and body.

For me it boiled down to a conference with a personnel officer one day, on Guam, and he suggested that, as requested by the commander of the new outfit I was in (an outfit disgustingly fresh from the States), I move into the quarters of the steward mates, who were all Negro. I was a pharmacist's mate and until then had shared a tent with two other pharmacist's mates who had been transferred into the outfit with me. I refused to move, was given a speedy court-martial for disobeying orders, and summarily sentenced to five days' bread and water in a Marine brig. But there were formalities. I had to be checked to see if my health was good. I was running a temperature, malaria, and they dumped me in the sick bay. However, to circumvent my suspended sentence, they came to take my temperature in the morning, when fevers usually run low. They found my temperature near normal and hauled me off to the brig, where dry shaves were the order of the day. We had to walk three miles for our bread and water, even the guys who were chained together. We had one cigarette after each "meal," had it standing in line. Some of us became dizzy from them, spaced as they were. Japanese prisoners of war gave us cigarettes and candy. Naturally, most of the American prisoners were Negro.

So, I knew the feeling.

"I don't give a damn," the second airman repeated. I was plunging through panic. By the time I wrote of my trip to Grand Forks, this kid might have already blown his top.

My guide said, "You get a traffic violation in town and your picture gets in the paper, but not a white airman."

"Please, can't you do something?" the second airman said,

with the air of one who is prepared to take matters into his own hands.

"I'll do what I can," I said, shaking his hand and feeling as useless as hell. Jesus Christ, what do I tell my sons now?

Kennedy would do something, my guide said, when we got back into the car. "When he was out here, he reached over people to shake my hand." He looked at me as though daring me to dispute his statement.

"I'm sure he would do something," I said.

He was through for the day and we drove to my motel and opened a bottle. I placed a call to Bob Johnson at *Jet,* told him what I had learned, and he promised to get a man up there as soon as possible. "Not right away," he said, "can't, but tell them cats up there to hang on in there, hear?"

It was night now and it closed fiercely over the town. We drove along the straight stretch of road into town, to my guide's home. He lived in a ramshackle building; the rooms he and his wife shared were matchboxes; the ceilings and walls were done in cheap paint over buckling walls. The place came furnished, but the furniture must have been carted from England at the height of the Victorian period; there was hardly room to pass between the chair and couch in the living room.

"What do you pay?"

"Eighty-five a month, on my salary. And we looked for seven months."

The chitlins were good, but we ate off a card table. "So we can fold it up and make believe that there's more room than we actually have," the young wife said. She was a nurse in town, and hated it. "I've been here for months, but they still treat me like I'm some kind of freak."

Just as we finished, four Negro airmen in civilian clothes came in.

"Where you guys going?" my guide asked.

"To a movie," one of them said. "Do you know, we've never been to a movie in this town. We don't even know if they'll let us in or not, but we're going to try. Safety in numbers, you know." They all grinned. As they filed out the door, one turned and said, "Sure hope you can do something, Mr. Williams."

"Man, he's already started," my guide said with a laugh. "He called *Jet* two hours ago."

"Yeah?"

"Yeah!"

So much faith in *Jet?* I don't know. When they went out, they went out smiling; they hadn't come in that way. A man in Athens once asked me why black Americans had their own magazines. Weren't they Americans too? And I had to reply that too often the black American does not see his image in the American press—thus, Negro publications.

The airman agreed to take me around the town, and we drove through streets filled with Christmas shoppers. In a club we found another group of Negro airmen. This was one of the clubs that would serve them. "Is this another safety group?" I asked.

"Goddamn right," one of them said. The club was a dark and dingy place, and as we were about to leave, some musicians climbed on the stand and started placing chairs. One looked like a Negro.

"That guy," my guide said, "has been passing for an Indian for years, they tell me. He gets along with everybody. Doesn't he look like a brother to you?"

He did indeed.

Later my guide took me around the town, pointing out places whose windows ordinarily carried signs that read: *Indians and Colored not allowed*. But it was dark; the signs were small, and I didn't see them. Only the places where I was told they were. As we walked, we came upon a pinch-faced woman pushing a baby in a stroller. She slowed, as if demanding that we move off the sidewalk. When we didn't she drew up her skinny frame and came straight ahead, looking neither right nor left. The stroller struck my ankle as she passed. I thought, You little bitch!

We passed beneath the Christmas lights strung along two or three short blocks in the center of Grand Forks. Merry Christmas.

The rains had returned by morning. The land along the way was still flat, and jet black. The vistas were broken only by signs of life—house or cabin, cattle and horse, an occasional car—but seldom by the living themselves. By now I had become aware of people turning in their cars when they passed me or I passed them. I had noticed it coming out of Duluth, but it hadn't mattered, not even when they pointed. Now, and perhaps it had to do with the SAC base, I found myself suddenly tired of it all, the grins, the double takes.

One man, his car filled with children, turned to grin and point at me. His car suddenly spurted dust as it veered off the narrow road. I watched him in the rear-view mirror as he skidded back on the highway, and I felt nothing for him or for the kids, not hate, not joy.

I passed through Minot without trouble. The airman at Grand Forks had told me that the citizens there walk up to you and ask what you are doing in their town. Back off the road were groves of blue spruce, northern crown, and Lombardy poplars.

Once again the land slanted upwards; the car hummed as it moved steadily up the hills, which were becoming mountains. Montana, the land of the big sky. The rain stopped and the entire sky became blue and unimaginably vast. It *was* the land of the big sky. Buttes and mesas, wadis and jagged mountains reared upwards from the earth, itself sun- and wind-scorched a livid brown. After the plains, I exulted in the climb, the curves, the massive shifting panorama. Sometimes, achieving a plateau, I romped across it, seeing solitary oil pumps dipping into the ground and out like some misshapen beast at some forbidden orgy. And once coming through a pass, the sun burning fiercely, high in the blue sky, I had the feeling that the car was aimed directly toward it. I went up and up and up, and as I topped the crest, I had the wild, joyous feeling that if I lowered the window I could reach up and touch the sun, bring it down and fondle it in my lap. The feeling went as quickly as it had come, for I had topped the crest and sped down the other side.

I was still in some kind of secret, bubbling elation when I pulled into a gas station in a half-mile-long town named Wolf Point. The attendant buoyed up my mood with a big smile and the way he moved to check the car.

When he was finished he asked, still smiling, "Playing in town tonight?"

"I'm afraid I don't understand," I said, feeling that his question and my presence, put together, amounted to something terribly Negro.

He hastened to say, "I thought you were with the Harlem Globetrotters. I read they would be in town tonight. I'm sorry."

So he knew that he had goofed. The conclusion he had jumped to was based on color, had to be, for I stand only five feet eight inches tall. But I suppose it is a mark of progress to be mistaken for an athlete rather than an entertainer or a musician.

But my day was not complete. Later I walked into a motel. A teen-age girl came out of a rear room and stopped dead when she saw me. I asked for a room as if I hadn't noticed. She hesitated, still on the balls of her feet, and then said, "All right."

I pushed it, asking if my room were downstairs or up, and when she said up, I asked for one down. I didn't feel like lugging the gear all the way up and then down again the next morning.

The man I assumed to be her father wouldn't talk to me the next morning. When I asked questions, he rattled his paper, reddened behind the neck, and continued reading. I placed more faith in his daughter; it was a good thing she had been at the desk and not her father. Perhaps they had quarreled.

Late in the afternoon, after turning south and coming through Great Falls and Missoula, where I had seen a group of Shriners riding the streets in Go-Karts, I found a camp site in the Bitterroot Range. I had crossed the Continental Divide at Rogers Pass, and there had been snow. There was snow in Lolo Pass, over 5,000 feet up. But the air was clean and pure, and there were no people except a few deer hunters, and they were all on the way in. I dug out the cold-weather gear and dressed, then got a few dry twigs, gassed some wood, and put the instant soup and coffee on, next to a can of sausages. I loaded the rifle and the shotgun to capacity, tossed more wood on the fire, then turned the ignition on so the car could warm up. Then laying out the seat cushions, I spread out the sleeping bag and opened it. Now the cognac. Peace, dammit, no people.

I slept late, and when I awoke, frost lined the windows of the car. I hastened into the front seat to get the engine warm. Over coffee, I thought about the hunting. I had not secured a license. And suppose I did find a roadway to hell and gone and at the end of it there were deer or elk; suppose I were lucky enough to down one—then what? Who would help me dress it and load it? And even if I did that alone, whom would I give it to? It didn't make sense. But I started looking for that kind of road anyway, and finding it, I became lost, late in the afternoon. I knew generally where the west was, because the sun had started its downward run and the mountains were already plunging from a cold green to a colder, more royal purple. I saw a small house sitting on a mud road and I drove out and knocked on the door. A man opened it. He was tall, in his thirties, and was wearing a gray ten-gallon hat and heavy plaid shirt. A great German shepherd crouched behind him. I liked the way he opened the door. He listened to me, gave me directions, and returned to his fire or his dinner or both. We had talked man to man. There had been none of the other things there, the stare, the smile of amusement that meant "What brings *you* to our town?"

In 15,000 miles of travel, I was refused accommodations only once, and that was not outright. It happened in Lewiston, Idaho. I had come through the pass with night falling fast. When a sign said "Caution 25 M.P.H." that is exactly what it meant. The pass, used by Lewis and Clark in 1805 (after the Indians, of course), twists and turns, doubles back upon itself, stretches out deceptively, angles sharply, curves again into a drop or another rise. The driving had been bad enough, but the ice and snow had tripled the hazards.

As I came into town, I had the nagging feeling that this was going to be my night, that now that I was pooped and with all defenses gone, someone would reach back and let me have it in the mouth with their foot. I couldn't rid myself of the feeling as I drove down the main street and crossed the bridge.

It was a Saturday night. There were not many cars in the lot of the motel, but then I didn't think there would be. In the fall and winter the busiest times for motels are during the week, when the businessmen are on the road. The woman at the motel told me there were no singles left. She was dressed in black, with jewelry, as though she were getting ready to go to a dance or a party. In a room to the rear of the desk I could see a young man. He leaned toward another man, I gathered, who was out of sight. They were watching *Gunsmoke.*

"Then a double or a family unit," I said. I had to get to bed. I wasn't even hungry. She looked directly at me then, her rhinestones glittering wildly. Retreating to the rear room, she addressed the man out of sight in a low voice, at first, and I was unable to hear them. Another customer came in at that moment, a white man, and he stood with all the assurance in the world. There would be a room for him anywhere, any time. Inside, amid gunfire, the woman raised her voice suddenly and sharply, and I heard quite clearly: "Well, tell me. Do you want him or don't you?"

He didn't want me. The woman came out of the room, walking very fast, her face set. "I'm sorry, but we have no more vacancies." I had been studying the racks where the registration cards were kept; there were only four slips in them. I took a deep breath to block the words that wanted to come out. Once they began, I knew, they would pull me along and I would not have been satisfied until I had had that whole place in pieces. And yet, feeling the anger, there was room for something else: pity for the woman who was the tool. Now she dropped her head and turned to the new-comer. He would have, at least in my presence, a reservation, of course.

For an instant, striding toward the car, I felt as though I were plunging helplessly down through black space, with nothing to grab hold of. I have been in some cities of the world, alone, with no one to call, let alone speak to, and did not feel as frightened or as alone as I did that night. The feeling was underlined by the rain and wind sweeping from the foothills of the mountains. I turned the car around on screeching tires, fully intending to try every hotel and motel in town. I sped across the street to another motel, jammed on the brakes, and bounded out, belligerent as hell.

And do you know what happened? The clerk couldn't sign me in fast enough.

The gray skies that had covered me nearly the entire north-plains route melted before sunshine. I sat in a parking lot in Walla Walla, Washington, and basked in the warmth. I was waiting for Bill Gulick, whom I had called, and he was tak-ing me to his home. I had never met Bill and I had never read any of his books. Now I sat feeling devilish. Did he know that I was Negro? What would be his reaction? Over the phone he had invited me to stay at his home. Would he suddenly find some excuse now? It would be good to see; it would make up for the night in Lewiston.

Bill Gulick, happily, disappointed me. He gladdened me too. He pulled into the lot and looked over at my car, the only one there. He got out, walked over, and didn't bat an eyelash over his wise blue eyes. I followed him out to his

home and met his wife, Jeanie. Both have dark hair and
blue eyes; Bill's hair is graying. He is stocky and ruddy and
would have made a good baseball catcher, and was, I think,
until he was hit with polio. But that didn't keep him out. He
bounded back and has become over the years a good, selling
writer. Although his settings are mostly in the West, he
doesn't like to be considered a Western writer. His last book
was *Hallelujah Train*.

The Gulicks have a small place outside town. They don't
like cities anymore, having lived in many of them from the
Atlantic to the Pacific. From the yard I could see an occasional house, but mostly miles and miles of green fields. In a
nearby one, I saw a pheasant speeding through the under-
brush, and thought about the guns in the car. Bill is like me
when it comes to hunting; he goes with only one man, his
brother, or alone. The man I usually go with is in Africa,
which means I go alone or not at all. Standing on the front
lawn, we stared at the brown, soft folds of the mountains.
Bill said they were very treacherous. Hunters could go up in
clear weather and in a couple of hours become lost in snowstorms. I thought about the motel in Lewiston and wondered
aloud how a man who lived close to the mountains and had
them in view all day could possibly be mean. I said it without making reference to what had happened.

"Maybe it's living near the mountains that makes him
mean. He becomes a very small and insignificant thing. Maybe it bothers him." It didn't bother Gulick.

In the afternoon we went on a trip around town, to the
site of the Whitman Massacre of 1847, to Whitman College,
and to Ice Harbor Dam. There, peering down in the locks,
I saw, for the first time in my life, salmon swimming up-
stream. Perhaps it was the company of Bill and Jeanie, but
I took a child's delight in seeing the fish. We passed along
the Columbia River and through wheat fields. "What do the
farmers here think of the wheat deal?"

"They're not paying too much attention to it. They've got
markets in the Orient. Soft wheat they grow here, and it's
used for noodles and such. The other is hard wheat for
bread and pastries."

While we had drinks later, Bill and I discussed that awful
disease of writers, jealousy. We discarded that very quickly.
I asked if he had heard anything of the Abominable Snow-
man of northern California. He laughed and told me how in

researching his books he often ran into stories of big Indians who, when investigations were launched, did not exist. "People used that big-Indian legend to scare their children into behaving. But the kids got wise. Sometimes they went out and made a pair of big feet themselves and tracked through the mud and snow, scaring the hell out of the parents. To my knowledge, no one has ever actually seen a giant."

Then we ran down some of the giants in legend—Goliath, the one Jack killed, the ones lurking in *Beowulf*, in the medieval tales, and so on. What I liked most about conversations with Bill was that not once did we discuss civil rights. I understand that most people are concerned with it and that they would like to discuss it with Negroes. But this happens almost to the exclusion of any other topic the Negro may also be interested in. To put it bluntly, most white people tend to assume that if a Negro knows nothing else, he knows civil rights. Bill Gulick did not demean me so; he treated me as another guy, another writer. But it had to end, and it ended when I placed a call to Seattle.

I had selected a motel at random, and when I talked to my contact there, I asked if he would make a reservation for me.

He said, "Frankly, John, I don't think you'll be welcome there."

Gulick was in the other room and could not see my face. I was glad. I said into the phone, "Would you reserve somewhere for me, then, and I'll call you as soon as I get to town."

"Righto, John."

He was very blithe about the whole business, gallingly blithe, as if that was the way things were and we could do nothing about them. After the call, Bill and I resumed our writer's talk, but at least on my part, with much less fervor. I was thinking about the next day. Bill put me up in the room where he works. The small brown desk with the office-model typewriter sat ready. Behind, on the wall, were his working tools, and over my bed, his bookshelves. The place where I work is foolishly sacred to me. I get nervous when my boys sit at the desk and peck on the typewriter. If any visitor goes near my desk or starts peering at papers, I automatically say, "Here! What are you doing?" But there I was in Bill's room, his work space, manuscript in progress and all. I felt very special.

When I left Walla Walla I came through the bristling, snow-speckled Cascades, whizzed past Whisky Dick Mountain, crept up through Snoqualmie Pass, and so arrived on the outskirts of Seattle.

After I checked into the motel the first thing I did was to call Ola, my mother, who lives in Los Angeles.

"Where are you?" she asked.

I was sheepish when I told her; I hadn't written or called since leaving New York. She knew only that I was coming.

"How did it go?"

"All right."

"Did you get to Mississippi, boy?"

"Yes."

"Did you get my letter before you left New York?"

"No. Was it about something important?"

"Well, I just wanted to tell you how to get along in the South. You know how you are." (She should have seen me.) "But you did all right, I guess. No trouble?"

"No." I wondered if I would be the same way when my children are grown and almost 40 years old.

"Now, how long before you'll be down this way?"

I told her.

"For how long?"

"A week."

"Only a week," she said. "I thought you said two weeks."

I couldn't begin to explain to her how vast I had found this country driving around it alone, to tell her that 300 to 400 miles a day took a terrible toll of one's energy. "Baby, I just can't help it."

I hung up. It was time for me to meet my Seattle contact.

Robert Doll just knew that I would be interested in civil rights. I did not know him; he was a friend of a friend. At his home, we settled at the bar, which overlooked Lake Washington and Seattle. "What do you hear about Dick Nixon?" he asked.

As a matter of fact, I had heard less about him in the plains than anywhere else. I had noticed more Goldwater bumper stickers, however. We chatted about a variety of things until the people he had invited to dinner arrived. One was a student at the University of Washington, a young, plump girl. And there was a couple, the wife American and the husband Swedish, and then Donaldson Wade, a Negro and principal of a white school in Seattle. He had grown up with Robert in the Midwest.

We talked about housing, education, and employment; there was a crisis in each. I had forgotten that whites on the West Coast are called "Caucasians." The adjective took the edge off the conflict inherent in the terms "black" and "white."

Now, I listened to Peg, the co-ed, who told of dating Negro youths. The couple told of their daughter dating Negro boys. Wade told of his son dating "Caucasian" girls. I stared through the glass doors at the lights of Seattle.

What were Goldwater's chances in the Northwest, I wanted to know.

Robert said, "The Republicans have no one. Goldwater's a whipping boy, expendable. You just can't get the fire started with him. They'll groom for sixty-eight."

I turned to the co-ed and asked, "What do you think of America today, as it is at this moment; what do your friends think of it?"

The room fell silent. She started and stopped.

"Start anywhere," I said.

Perhaps it was the wrong time and place. She didn't know how to say what she thought of America. Sulking a little, I withdrew from her and concentrated on Wade, who was talking in dollar signs: how much his son's car cost, how much it cost his family for last summer's vacation. I listened and watched him. He was well groomed, held a good position in that troubled city, knew Robert Doll very well, and yet I believe he was uneasy there. I glanced at Peg. She shrugged and smiled. Still nothing to say. I could have told her about America, how big it is, and how much space there was, and how, when they dig us up 5,000 years from now, we, or rather, our remains will be found like those of the ancient peoples, along the coasts, rivers, and great inland seas. And should someone stumble over a place like Wolf Point, or Panther Burn, they will consider the people who lived there quaint and different altogether, like the "C" or "X" peoples of the Sudan. And they will write, those archeologists, that despite advanced technology, the habits of the people on this continent were not vastly unlike those of other people the world over. Pity, they will write, that they did not use that technology of which they were so proud to make all the land they possessed more livable.

". . . see why you want to send your boy to a Negro school, Donaldson," Robert was saying. The food was just about gone and we were drinking again.

Wade wanted his son to "know his people" better. It would cost him a pretty penny, but he had to do it. Living in a society in which most of his dates were "Caucasians," and many of his male friends too, the boy would never find out that he belonged to the whole and not just to one or the other.

Say something, girl, I thought, glancing at Peg again. This country is yours, practically, yours, Wade's son's, your whole new generation. What do you *think* of America?

Finally, the night ended. Robert drove me back to the motel. "What did you think of Wade?"

"Not much."

The coup de grace for passenger travel in American railroads is but a matter of time now. The production of the Boeing 727, the short- to medium-range jet liner, is aimed unerringly at the railroad industry's jugular. On the next cross-country trip I take, if I take one at all, I may notice a complete absence of long-haul passenger trains. The 727's are coming off the line at Boeing's Renton, Washington, plant.

I went through the plant thinking, as I watched the workers, that factories are all the same. There were a couple of goldbricks in the corner, watching over their shoulders for the boss; there was the smell of sweat-stained denims and the odor of stale sandwiches and coffee, all mixed with the clean, eager scent of metal being scored or shaved, drilled or riveted. Up on the catwalk the workers swarmed over the planes, passing them from one position to another through the whole of that huge building until, finally, the ship was pushed outside for further work and painting.

A 727 had just returned from a trip around the world, a publicity ride. There were several on the line, brightly painted, shedding the steady rain. The names of the airlines that had ordered them were painted on the sides. The 727 has its engines mounted on the tail in the rear. Of all the jet planes, the Caravelle is the quietest because its engines are mounted rearward, but next to the 727, the Caravelle looks less sturdy. Essentially a short-hop jet, the 727, especially if the fares are at all comparable to railroad fares, may help change the complexion of America; the whistle-stop may come back. Any city that can afford to build a runway only a mile long and a terminal can be in business.

I did not see more of the great beauty of the Northwest because of the rain. I paused in Portland long enough to have dinner and a talk with friends, and then started south to San Francisco.

The rain followed me down the Oregon coast and into California, where I took the Redwood Highway for the sheer grandeur of it. The road twists and turns so that one moment I was in sight of the Pacific Ocean, clambering in a wild white froth up the shoreline, and the next I was cast thousands of years into time by the gigantic sequoias, so tall and thick that they blocked out what was left of the gray daylight. Once, at Meggido, in Israel, I stood in the ruins of Solomon's temple. Then I stared down the long tunnel behind the stables. No one else was there, and thus no one joined me going through the tunnel, which had served both as an escape route and a water reservoir. The feeling I had then was at once eerie, exultant, and goose-pimpling. I had to consider *time,* time past and time passing. I had the same feeling driving around the feet of those giant trees. Here the feeling of power of a good car fades; I had to travel slowly to take the curves safely, and in so doing, I made a studied obeisance and felt insignificant and pensive. What was the earth like when those trees first took root? How I envied them—centuries old, they still lived, rooted atop great mountains, monuments to themselves. I would die, my sons and their sons would die, and so on down the line, but the trees would live on.

It was while passing through the Redwood Forest that I damned all truck drivers to hell. Until that day I had always found truck drivers to be skillful and courteous on the road. In Kentucky, I was about to pass a truck after the driver had given me the signal, but as I pulled out to go around, he swung over in front of me to keep me from passing because, up ahead, a car had darted out of a driveway. The Redwood Highway is narrow. Frequent turnouts have been cut into the side of rocks along the road to permit slow traffic to pull in and allow faster traffic to move on. Not so for the great trucks that rushed along. They clattered downhill, pushed by their cargoes; then they charged you, threatened to crush you or run you off the edge of the mountain. If they were ahead going uphill, they crept on, refusing to pause in the turnouts to let the traffic piling up behind pass. I was almost a chattering madman when I arrived in San Francisco.

My mother had told me, when I called her from Seattle, that a woman friend of mine in San Francisco was delaying her marriage until I arrived there, so I could give her away. My brother, Joe, was flying up from Los Angeles to attend the wedding. As I picked my way through town to a hotel, I could see that San Francisco was still changing. The whorehouses and nightclubs that used to line Filmore Street were gone. In their places were new superroads to speed the driver from one section of the city to another. I passed near Treasure Island and thought, as I always do when near there, of Walter Timothy Farrell.

He was from Brooklyn. We had met on Treasure Island just days before leaving for the South Pacific. Together we explored the wonders of the island, which had been a fairground site. We sailed on an old Dutch vessel, the *M.S. Japara,* and got separated in the Solomons.

Some months later I had one letter from him saying that he had returned to the States on leave and was being assigned to the aircraft carrier *Bunker Hill.* I read the letter with great bitterness. Had rigid segregation not existed, I too might have been home on leave and assigned to a combat vessel, instead of island hopping and pulling a steady twenty months. But Wally was white; it made all the difference in the world. But around Easter, 1945, off Okinawa, the *Bunker Hill* came under furious Kamikaze attack and Walker Timothy Farrell was killed. He volunteered at sixteen and was not nineteen when he died.

I cannot visit San Francisco without thinking of him. He was my friend. Once we walked through the Negro section of Oakland and stopped at a bar. The bartender wouldn't serve him because he was white. I remember his strange, puzzled look, made even more strange by the greenish cast of the overhead fog lights.

On this visit I checked into a hotel, called the bride-to-be, and fell off to sleep. The next morning, the day of the wedding, the bride-to-be phoned to tell me that she decided not to get married. She was a slight young woman, given to deep fits of depression. She used to baby-sit for us in Syracuse when she was a teen-ager. I had known her in New York for a couple of years, during which time she came to be very much like a sister. As far as I could determine, she had an inferiority complex that caused her great personal grief. Yet in her chosen profession, nursing, she was among the best.

When Joe arrived and heard the news, he said, "Well, tough, baby. So what else is new? Let's celebrate. When anybody makes a decision these days, it's worthy of a celebration." It has always seemed to me, these past few years, that my brother, six years my junior, is as old as I. He doesn't mind that I have killed him off in two novels; he thinks that is very funny. He was the first in my family to accept my wish to be a writer. I feel shame or guilt whenever I shake his hand; it is so big and hard, and mine, once also hard and callused, has become soft.

In a halfhearted way we did celebrate. Cannonball Adderly and Mose Allison were in town; the lines were long in front of the North Beach clubs where they were playing. My brother and I, the young woman who had backed out of her marriage, and my date—a young Negro who had adopted a Korean orphan—moved along the crowded street, darted in and out of heavy traffic creeping up the hill to North Beach. I was reminded of Eighth and MacDougal streets in Greenwich Village. Once I looked at my little friend, who, if things had gone right, would have been a bride at that very moment. I wondered how she felt; I wondered how her boyfriend felt. I was sorry for both. At evening's end my brother took her home, and with some relief my date and I moved on to Oakland.

I was curious as to why she had adopted the Korean orphan. "We just fell in love," she said. I was also interested in the new, liberal adoption laws. There was a time when a single person could not adopt a child. But since orphans keep coming, orphans and the unwanted, someone has to take them. Adoption agencies are beginning to learn, finally, that "ideal" families are rare indeed.

At a Negro club in Oakland we were given a very bad table toward the rear. The tables near the bandstand were being held open for the white patrons who drifted in. We complained and got a table that was better, but still not good enough for our tastes, and we left. I dropped her off at her home, to her son, knowing I'd never see her again. That upset me somewhat, for I had found her a nice person, one who cared, one who did something about caring.

Later that night, my brother and I, as brothers will do, opened a bottle, drank, and talked. I hadn't seen him for two years. The next time it might be five. Who could tell?

If Negroes in Detroit claim their votes put the mayor in office, Negro San Franciscans ascribe the astonishing win over Harold Dobbs by John F. Shelley, a Democrat, to their voting power or at least to a racial situation. According to the San Francisco *Chronicle,* Shelley had "no single important paper behind him." But Dobbs "was the careful precise Republican in a city which had not elected a Democrat as Mayor for 55 years."

As Election Day neared, the six restaurants owned by Dobbs were picketed by the Direct Action Group of the United Freedom Movement, demanding that he integrate the workers. Dobbs replied that 30 of his 245 employees were Negro. The Direct Action Group acknowledged that Negroes worked for him, but were not in "visible" positions and therefore discriminated against. Both candidates had had to deal with rising tensions. "One candidate hammered at fear of violence," the *Chronicle* continued, "fear of racial overlap, fear of the stranger in our midst.

"The other spoke of 'compassion and equality.'

"Quite possibly the single most critical utterance of the campaign was Mr. Dobbs' observation that if Mr. Shelley were elected Mayor, San Francisco would indeed become another Birmingham.

"This was a desperate statement, and its failure is now obvious."

When the polls closed, 120,560 people had voted for Shelley and 92,627 for Dobbs. The population of San Francisco is about 800,000.

Actually the "stranger" in their midst was no stranger at all; he had long ago made himself felt in San Francisco. William Alexander Leisderdorff, U. S. Subconsul to Mexico in 1845, was city treasurer and a member of the first city council. He was a Danish mulatto. Mary Ellen "Mammy" Pleasant, a civil-rights stalwart, raised $30,000 for rifles for John Brown's raid on Harpers Ferry. These two persons might have been considered "strangers," but more than one hundred years have elapsed since then. And Negroes are still considered "strangers" in San Francisco?

As usual, it came time to leave. This time it was not so bad, for my brother, Joe, helped with the driving. I wasn't alone anymore. This part of California was not as staggeringly beautiful as the north. The entire valley was under cultivation and now we began to see the communities of Mexicans who labor throughout the San Joaquin Valley, many at starvation wages.

Some hours later we hit the Los Angeles freeway system. Joe was driving, and he kept lifting his nose and smiling, as a horse smelling home. Ahead of us, one car passing another hooked bumpers. Both cars flashed around in a blur of metal and glass. Joe swung out and we went around, seeing the white startled faces still jerking and snapping. We left them, as other freeway riders left them, to their lawsuits and X rays, wrecking trucks and recriminations.

It was Sunday, November 17, when we arrived finally in the driveway of my mother's home. The lights were on, and Ola and my stepfather, Albert, stepped out onto the porch. We went through the formal things, the handshakes, the embraces. "Thought you'd never get here," Ola said. "Waited dinner for you and then had to eat. Got hungry. Hello, Joseph Williams," she said to Joe fondly. He always was her pet.

"Later for that, baby, I'm hungry," Joe said, striding toward the kitchen.

"Oh, I fixed a few little ol' chitlins," my mother said, as if apologizing. I am very fond of chitlins, and she knows it. My first night out of the service we celebrated with a large chitlin and potato-salad dinner. Now she turned to me, "But you don't like chitlins, do you?" She pinched me. "Does you, boy?" Ola believes my tastes have changed since I began writing, or at least she always tests to see if they have.

It has been a long road for her, accepting my wanting to write. When I was young, she made one of her rare concessions—after all, I would surely change my mind about writing in a few years. She gave me a copy of Keats' poems bound in leather. There were so many things between the time she gave me the gift and the time I actually sat down to write that she was quite startled to find that I was still involved in "creating." Her letters to me invariably expressed with little subtlety the hope that things were going well, and she did not mean writing. At other times I would open her letters to find a five- or ten-dollar bill, smuggled away from Albert, cutting back on his poker funds and cutting down on her own little relaxation, playing the horses. But Ola always recognizes that I have inherited some of her traits. She is stubborn as hell, and I am afraid I am too. We are both chiefs, in a sense, in a wigwam that sometimes tends to be very small. She never has had courage enough to ask disdainfully, as some of my other relatives have, "Are you *still* messing around with that writing?"

I feel many things when I visit Ola. A great pride that she is my mother, old hen that she is sometimes, and I feel guilty. We have always sweated for our money in my family, and bent our backs, and often held our tongues because we had to eat and feed those younger than ourselves. When dawn breaks, I may be turning over in bed, but I know that my mother and stepfather are up, warming the car, having their first sleep-touched words before going off to work. My brother may already be at work since he heads up three departments. My sisters are up and at work. And there I lie. It doesn't matter that I may have worked until two in the morning. You cannot see a brain work; it doesn't smell of sweat and it doesn't wear out as quickly as a biceps. My body no longer is an instrument; my mind is. I am not saying that they do not use their minds on their jobs. I am saying that their presence, their *bodily* presence, is required there, more than their minds.

There have been times when I think Ola understands my feelings better than I do myself. For example, when I arrived, the den had been cleared out for me to work in, and a heater had been hooked up to offset the chill of the Los Angeles mornings. It was her way of telling me that it was all right, my divorce from their way of earning a living.

I wanted to rest the next day, but couldn't. I was up early in the morning—shortly after Ola and Albert had left for work—and out strolling the lawn, looking up and down the block for changes that might have occurred since my last visit. There had been some. My parents had been the first colored people to buy in the block. But by 1961, only four years after they had moved in, there were only three or four white families still there. Now they too were gone.

Sam's Deli had moved across the street and the New York *Times* had taken his corner for the printing of its Western edition. The fact that Sam was still on one of the four corners was comforting.

"I'd Walk a Mile for the Western Edition of the New York Times" read a bumper sticker. "We Shall Overcome" read another.

I was suddenly seized with the desire to prowl again and again through the empty house, as I used to do when I was a child in Syracuse and had gone off to school only to double back through the alleys and spend the afternoon walking through room after room, touching things I had already touched a million times. Still holding a cup of coffee, I went out to the garage and climbed to one of the lofts, pulling around for old books I might have left there from my short and sorry stay in Los Angeles, a city I despise with all my being. I did find one or two books that once held some value for me, but no longer did.

I spent that first day browsing and doing nothing except getting bored with myself. Ola rushed in from work and prepared dinner, an unusual thing for her because she believes, and rightly so, that if she's been working all day, the one who is at home should prepare the meal. So, she had changed a great deal.

Although I disliked the city when I lived there, I had made a few friends. I visited them, a publicist, a psychologist, an architect and his wife and family. The publicist (who, incidentally, is also vice-president of a banking firm) is Marj Greene, who for a number of years now has been trying to break into film writing without success. The fact that she studied with Bresson in Paris is not the important thing; the color of her skin is. It was most painful for me to listen to her. There is something too awful, too dizzying, for a person to describe in detail his torture, the pain of his wounds. And when you sit in a restaurant overlooking the sea at Malibu, the hurt is beyond description.

Rafe Roig was the architect. He worked on the Air Force Academy and now designs the silos for those missiles that are pointed at Russia. I couldn't help but pause (I was eating cheesecake his wife, Jackie, had made with beer) and stared at him.

And I visited another newsman.

On my way, I passed Beverly Drive, and oh, I wanted to slam on the brakes and turn into it, prowl up the street to the house where I once worked as a butler. The house had been huge, with two wings, a great dining room, cork floors. My own room and private bath were the epitome of luxurious living. The madame had given me white jackets for serving, and gray jackets to wear while dusting and cleaning the place. There were three children, two of whom were snots I had to drive to Beverly Hills High each morning. One night the teacher of one of the children was invited to dinner. She drove up in an old, rattling car. Young and nervous, she was very much ill at ease all night, not only because of the grand splash the madame was putting on, but because madame was trying to intimidate her into giving the kid a good grade, which he did not deserve. Once I looked at the teacher and gave her a half smile. Courage, baby! The next time the madame was looking the other way, she gave me a wink.

I hated that job even before I began it, but I could find nothing else. I had been unemployed in California for an astronomical number of days. The day I started, the cook looked at me and said, "You ain't never buttled before, have you?"

"Oh yes I have," I told him. I needed that job, which only made me despise it the more.

"No you ain't," he said with a knowing smile.

"Aw, man, later for you," I told him. Ola had given me a few quick courses on setting the table, picking up and serving. As the day wore on and my hatred grew, the lessons were forgotten and at dinner I panicked.

"Man, help me with this goddamn table—please."

He laughed, how he laughed. "I knowed it," he said. But if it hadn't been for him I would have lost the job that night. Memories. You can't drive in Los Angeles and have your mind on memories and survive.

Traffic was too heavy for me to stop at the place where I had worked, and I continued on to Hollywood to see Bob Kirsch, book editor of the Los Angeles *Times*. We spent a pleasant afternoon talking in his home high in the hills. We talked about many things, but Baldwin Hills stands out in my mind.

Baldwin Hills is a section of Los Angeles, fairly exclusive, into which Negroes were trying to move in 1961. The grapevine used by Negro domestics is a fantastic news service. In 1961 a friend of my mother was working in a Baldwin Hills home in which a group of women gathered one day to discuss the problem of Negroes moving into the area. "The niggers are coming!" was the way the woman described the meeting to my mother.

By 1964, on my trip, they had come. My mother's doctor had moved there but had had to guard his family with fire-arms. What his white neighbors still don't know is that the doctor has hunted on safari in East Africa and is a crack shot. My personal advice would be to let that Negro alone.

I went to see the doctor because I wanted to see how Ola was coming along; she had complained about a couple of heart attacks.

"To my knowledge," the doctor said, "your mother hasn't had a single coronary. She has hypertension."

"She worries too much, about all of us, and all the time," I said, suddenly amused. That old faker! What Negro in America doesn't have hypertension? And on top of that Ola does worry. Unless she reads this, she will never know that I knew she wasn't as bad off as she said she was. Perhaps we just need to let her know more that we love her. Ours isn't a very demonstrative family; you could be away ten years and return home, and someone would say, "So what's new?"

I looked at the doctor and could imagine him with one of those high-powered Magnums, knocking over elephants and white folks in the same motion. I hastened to assure him that between my brother and myself, we would arrange a trip back East during the summer to give Ola a rest.

Ola wasn't behaving like someone with a bad heart; she was planning a family dinner, a pre-Thanksgiving Day affair, since I would be on the road that day. I could hear her on the phone calling relatives and friends. Her lines were always the same: "I want you all to come to dinner Sunday. John-ny's here. My boy, Johnny, the writer. Yes. He's doing a little writing for"—and here she would pause for emphasis—"*the* 'Holiday' magazine. Yes, um-huh. All right, we'll look for you then."

One night she hung up grinning and checked off another name on her list. She asked Albert for a bourbon and said to me, "Who's picking you up tonight?"

"Tommy Davis. We're going to a basketball game."

"*The* Tommy Davis?"

"The ball player, yeah, Mother." Ola was never interested in baseball until the Dodgers moved to Los Angeles. Now, when they are on a losing streak, like everyone else she wears the same clothes or some item of clothing until they hit the win trail again.

"Boy," she said, "you sure got some highfalutin friends. What time's he coming?"

By the time Davis arrived, my entire family was there—my sister Helen and her two kids, Joe, Albert, and Ola, who had done a swift powdering job on her face and pulled up her skirt.

Tommy Davis has been the National League batting champion two years in a row; he is a left fielder with the Dodgers. He came in tall, grinning, pork pie hat askew, and shook hands all around. My nephew, Melvin, asked for an autograph and became so nervous that he couldn't find his pen. Helen drooled, and Joe ran him up and down with a cool, calculating eye.

At the Coliseum, as soon as people saw Davis, a buzz went up. As we passed through the door, a kid ran up and asked, "Are you Tommy Davis?"

"Yes," Davis said, and kept walking.

"You lie!" the kid screamed.

"Autograph, Tommy."

"Autograph, Tommy." Even in the stands pieces of paper were passed while we watched the St. Louis Hawks get beat by the Los Angeles Lakers. Davis introduced me to some of his friends with "This is John Williams. He's a famous writer."

And there was no place for me to run to avoid the questions that came up: "Oh, yeah? What've you written? Yeah?" You are not famous if nobody knows your name, obviously. There were times when I was introduced as a writer, and before my name was announced, someone would rush over and say, "You're James Baldwin!" It is a sad and cruel world.

I am always intrigued by the way professional athletes study one another. Davis talked about the "good moves," the "good hands," and the "tough eyes" of the players; he could see a play being set up even before the players were in position. After the game we went to the lockers and picked up Davis' long-time buddy from Brooklyn, Len Wilkins, a backcourt man on the Hawks. The autograph seekers were still on Davis, and to a lesser extent on Wilkins. We retired to the dark confines of a nightclub. And who was working over the alto saxophone but an old acquaintance of mine, Willie Smith.

I first met him when I was the regimental bugler at Camp Robert Smalls at Great Lakes. After reveille came morning colors. After I played, the Ship's Company band, a cynical group of professional musicians who'd got caught in the draft, struck up the Star Spangled Banner. In that band were such jazzmen as Clark Terry, Jerome Richardson, and Willie Smith. While Davis and Wilkins talked about athletics, Willie and I talked about the old days and the fine musicians. Great sacks of flesh hung under Willie's eyes; he didn't look too well generally. "One nighters," he said, "and all that traveling. I'm just getting over being sick." He wiped his mouth. "And drinking too much, but there's nothing else to do when you're out there." He went back to the stand, a short plump man who could pass for white. He picked up his horn and played again; he was not the Willie Smith of old.

Tommy Davis and I parted on a pensive note; we had been talking about discrimination in professional athletics. "The hell with it," he said, "I'm going to win that title again next year."

John F. Kennedy was murdered in Dallas the next morning while I was shopping with my niece on Olivera Street. She tuned in her transistor, an instrument she is never without. Sobbing and broken voices rushed out of it; facts were helter-skelter and being altered every ten seconds.

"Close your mouth," I said to her. It was hanging open as if to trap flies.

Customers gathered near the small battered radio, stood shoulder to shoulder. One woman burst into tears on the spot. A Negro man was reported to have fled the scene. A Negro boy was reported to have seen two people struggling on an overpass along the route of the Kennedy car. "Negro" kept running through the reports like some lesser theme in a wild symphony, a theme that would at the finale become dominant.

My niece and I rushed back to the car, drove home, and turned on the television set. There, calmly holding his earphone was baggy-eyed Walter Cronkite, a man who often irritates me with his "personalized" reporting, but who that morning was a superb newsman. On the other channel, Frank McGee held forth as calm but more solemn. Both were a relief from the sobbing, hysterical radio reporters.

I had an appointment at Lightcraft of California, where Joe works, and I was to meet his boss again, Arthur Addis. In the parking lot of the plant, a man sweeping up the grounds asked me, "Is he dead?"

"No, but critical." That had been the last report.

The sweeper was a beefy man with a red face. He heaved a sigh of relief. "A salesman just came in and said he was dead."

At that moment the salesman came out. The sweeper said, "You were wrong, he's still alive."

"Like hell he is," the salesman said, getting into his car. "They just announced it officially. He's dead, like I told you." The sweeper turned away and passed his broom over the road.

Inside, Arthur Addis said, "John, a hell of a day this is." He was a tall, graying man who looked more like a fashion model than the president of a light-fixture manufacturing company.

Then Joe came out and took me to his departments. "It's all over, huh?"

"Yes."

"These damned people have lost their minds," he said.

I met his men in a kind of a daze and listened while Joe told them of the murder. Addis was walking around the plant in shock. "Joe, get the boys together. I want to talk to them."

Solemnly the men gathered in a cleared space. The machinery had been turned off. The men crept through corridors and from behind doors, their faces open and expectant.

"You've heard by now," Addis said, "that the President has been assassinated. I don't know what to tell you about this kind of hatred. I don't know how it's going to affect any of us. The best thing we can do is to be stable. Don't do anything in panic. Don't rush and take your money out of the bank. I'm not. There are Constitutional safeguards that will keep us stable. Don't panic. The New York Stock Exchange closed early to avoid panic. It's going to be a long weekend. For God's sake don't do anything foolish."

Addis turned and wandered off again. Joe took me by the arm and walked me to the car. "He's scared shitless," he said. "He's Jewish, you know, and maybe he can smell the pogrom coming. I'm scared too, man. It's the end of some-

thing. What? Tell me, you're the writer. What's it the end of
—liberalism?"

"Man, I don't know. You sense so many ugly things, so
big, so cumbersome, but effective as hell."

At home my niece wandered around the house saying,
"Uh, uh, uh." We watched a man-on-the-street show and
heard an interviewee say, "Some nigger did it." And later in
the afternoon my sister called to say that they had announced in her school over the public address system that a
Negro had murdered Kennedy. "Johnny, *we* would never
do a thing like *that!* We're not crazy like *they* are."

The reports of a Negro murderer seemed to prove how
fearful the white public is, at least in Los Angeles, of an
outbreak of racial violence. They expect it. When Lee
Harvey Oswald was taken in, a sense of relief seemed to
descend over the city, which had probably come closer to
a race riot than it dared dream. (I later learned that only
two or three other cities had been bombarded with such
racially slanted news.)

My mother kept rising from her deep well of disgust
("They just haven't got any sense") and grief ("That poor
boy riding with his wife on such a pretty day"), only to sink
into it again.

The family dinner that Sunday was a quiet affair, with
nearly everyone watching television. Lincoln had gone to his
burial by train, I thought, and Kennedy by jet; only the way
they travel varies. In this land of the free, this land given
to the bold slogan, since the Revolution Americans have
averaged one murdered President every forty-four and a
quarter years.

I watched my family reach across generations of poverty
and persecution and extend to the Kennedys deep and sincere sympathy. But a heavy air of irony remained, as if they
had known all along that disaster, sickness, hate, and anarchy
had to extend beyond them to encompass even the mightiest.
They have known all their lives—and perhaps it was bred
into them—that the power of government was an illusion
and that the people who made them aware of that fact had
to know it first. My family was fat and lean, tall and short,
and ranged from uncontaminated black to high yellow. They
knew that to be any degree of black was to scream down
the ages that the American dream of the beginning was not
yet fulfilled, and that when the opportunity to fulfill it has

been presented like the seats on a Ferris wheel, it has only been ignored.

The flag Ola had ordered flown at half-mast on the lawn was limp. My car was idling in the driveway, and it was loaded. There had been hints in our final words of time, what it gives and what it takes away. Ola and Albert are not young and have worked hard; knowing that they must go is not an easy thing to digest, with so much distance between us.

Two blocks down the empty street I saw a young woman walking up, her head covered with a veil as if she were just coming from Mass. She was Negro and I wondered if Kennedy's grief for the plight of my people had been as sincere as hers was for him.

Las Vegas was quiet that Monday after the murder, quiet and seedy and not at all the way I remembered it. The marquees listed Sammy Davis, Jr., and the Will Mastin Trio, Tex Benecke, Fats Domino, Edie Adams, Guy Lombardo, and a couple of baseball players, Bo Belinsky and Maury Wills, a teammate of Tommy Davis. Davis himself was slated to appear at a future date. An excellent dancer, Davis was cavorting backstage during preparations for a Bob Hope Show. Hope saw him and advised that he was the star on the show, not Davis.

Las Vegas was ugly but outside the town the land has a harsh, ridged beauty. Farther east, nestled among the con-figurations of an ancient and terrible diastrophism, was Lake Mead, created by the miles and tons of concrete that gave rise to Hoover Dam. Here the land is like the Negev or the northern section of Ethiopia—terribly warped, rising up from the ground to twist and spear toward the sky. In the center of that frozen violence was the dam itself. Never have I seen the hand of modern man so beautifully and precisely merged with the hand of nature. I stopped at the rim of the dam and gazed down. The top of my groin ached with the primeval instinct to hurl myself into space, through the cleanliness of it, far down into the slowly churning blue-green water or against the unending sweep of rust-colored concrete.

I had forgotten how strikingly lovely is northern Arizona. Massive snow-capped mountains, their shoulders spreading far across the land, rose thousands of feet into the sky.

Now, passing through the towns I saw the life-sized figures of Indians, all males. Was this the counterpart to the Mammy dummies of New Orleans? It was fitting, I think, that I stopped in Williams, Arizona, to eat. I did so with trepidation, for I had been through Arizona four times before and had always been refused service. I know Negroes who have had no trouble eating in that state, but for me, it was a question, perhaps, of always picking the bad spots.

I was eating when a cowboy came in. He smiled and said hello; I did not think he was speaking to me, but turning around, I saw that I was the only other customer in the place. He asked if I'd heard Lyndon Johnson's address on the radio and I said I hadn't. He said it had been good. I was eating rapidly now, suspecting that he was buttering me up for a lift; I like to pick my passengers. I nearly choked with eating so fast in order to get out of there before he was finished. But he beat me anyway, hopped off his stool saying, "See you, buddy," piled into a spanking new car, and drove away. My apologies, cowboy. My one excuse is that I was very wary because I've never before been able to eat in a public restaurant in your state.

Walking down a street in Gallup, New Mexico, I saw a Navaho coming toward me, smoothing his hair. As we passed he said, "How you making it, baby?"

I stopped dead still, I was so startled by that hipster's greeting. I would expect such a greeting in many places, but not in Gallup, not from a Navaho. I murmured in shock, "Fine, fine, thank you," and so, to him, at least, I became a square passing in broad daylight. The hippies have reached the West.

They say they reached the West through Denver, a city much dirtier than I remembered.

I came to the city from the south, through New Mexico, where, in Santa Fe, I had spent a quiet Thanksgiving watching the Detroit Lions and Green Bay Packers play to a 13–13 tie. The way to Denver lay through Raton Pass, and I drove through it with sunrays bouncing off the snow-covered slopes. And because there was snow, the thousands of acres of timber seemed unbelievably green. Slush and ice lay on the road, and in the most isolated place, I came around a curve and saw a sturdy frame house tucked behind a grove of spruce with smoke coming lazily out of its chimney.

Whenever I hit a pass such as that one, I moved slowly, being unused to the road. Most of the passes are hours long, and the longer I was in them, the more confidence I gained and thus more speed. I would zip past cars, pressing down hard on the accelerator and thinking that the people in the cars I passed were saying to one another, "Hot damn! Look at that guy from California take those curves, will you!" But to the natives who were used to taking the curves at 60, I was probably just another crawling California farmer.

The Colorado Plateau is a fantastic geophysical formation. For miles and miles, more than 5,000 feet up, it is flat— as flat as southern Ohio or Illinois. From every side you see the Rockies at mid-height. The air was clean and brisk; you could smell the snow on the peaks and the direct, enticing suggestive flirtation of nature: Come, make love to me, know me.

But love of the up-tramping slopes, the peaks, the passes, faded the closer I came to Denver and became involved in traffic, speedways, homes, buildings, the choking odor, so prominent after the mountains, of gas and oil, of hot mobile metal.

In the "Mile High City" a wonderful thing happened to me—again. I made new friends. But, I think, in a way I made friends all over America, for doors were opened to me and people talked.

There were the first few minutes of ornate politeness, of stiffness, of probing, and then the easy smile, the crossed leg as if inner gears had just been shifted from low to high, the offer of another drink. I sat easily in the house of Bob and Marilyn Hackworth; I sat at dinner, talked without strain to kids. In the probing there had come a relation-ship, and I was no longer black and they were no longer white, my hosts and their other guests. It is so goddamn good just to be people, with hosts who up until two hours earlier had never laid eyes on you and who are whipping up the meal in the kitchen. I think that eating together is still the basic expression of friendship.

I went with the Hackworths to the mountains, 5,000 feet farther up. We left on a clear, cold afternoon, and from the moment we left town, we curved up until we reached a ski resort. There, climbing out of the car, I became drunk and giddy with the altitude. What a marvelous explosion of space! We were in a kind of pit, and all around us the mountains rose powerfully, their narrowing necks collared with cedars and snow, except where the ski trails had slashed through them. Bob and Marilyn may have been used to the view, but I was transfixed and hated to leave. On the way through some of the old mining towns, I remarked to Bob that I expected to see an Indian in full headgear, his knees dug tightly into the sides of his pony, atop one of the bluffs.

"Do you?" he said, his tone surprised and glad.

"Okay, I feel foolish," I said.

"Oh, no," he answered, "I always feel that way, but I've never told anybody. Now I don't feel so silly."

It was one of those inner things, that shared feeling about Indians, and I guess friendships are built on such things.

We arrived in the old mining town of Central City just after dusk. It is a little town, with the present homes built atop old mining digs. The streets go up at a thirty-degree angle along the walls. The street lights are small, just barely glowing, and behind the counters of stores I could see silhouettes of people moving like ghosts. It is difficult to say what makes a man like a place. Perhaps here it was the guts to build again atop a mountain gone askew; perhaps the way the streets tilted or the wooden floors of the shops, the gaslight-like fixtures. One half hour at dusk on a Sunday afternoon and *wham*—love!

We took the back roads returning to Denver. Night had come and the shapes of the mountains were bold and raw; they seemed ready to open caves and let loose the dark secrets from the bottom of the world. I half expected to see, formed against the dark-blue sky, the shape of some monster inconceivable in the mind of man. But there was nothing until we rounded a curve and Bob came to an abrupt halt.

The headlights picked out a buck with a full head of antlers. "Look at that," Bob whispered. The buck's white tail flattened out behind him and quivered. He stared at the car, and then turned regally to look into the darkness. This from the heart of nature, at night—no monster, but a beautiful creature.

The buck turned back toward the car, lowered his head, and began to paw the road. I have read and heard of bucks who will charge a hunter, but until that night I had never seen it happen. Still pawing, he lowered his head until his points became menacing. And then, with a scrape of his hoofs on the roadway, he started toward us.

"He's charging!"

Bob forgot all about the horn. He, born of the near woods, with almost the physiognomy of an Indian and nearly as brown as one, forgot about the car horn, the instrument of automated man. He flung open the door of the little foreign car, leaped out, shouted, "Boo," and stamped his foot into the bargain. The buck recoiled in the middle of his charge and scampered up the slope. Only then did we see the doe; she had been waiting in the shadows.

"I didn't want him to hit the car," Bob explained, but I was still recalling the moment, not so much of the deer in the headlights, but of the deer charging.

Denver lay below us. The moon was up, fat and orange, and as we rushed downhill, it was below us; we would, it seemed, rendezvous with it at some point down among the passes that led to the city. We drove in silence, each with his own thoughts of the night. We arrived in the city, the silence continuing. What, after all, was there to say?

We were having dinner with other friends, Irene Dougherty and her daughter, Patti Cutler. But there were other people there, and it was stiff once again for a while—until dessert, when Irene, her gray hair shimmering in the candlelight, her cheeks redder than usual, came out of the kitchen with a candle-lit pumpkin pie and the entire table began to sing *Happy Birthday*. To me. A stranger wandering about the country. I did not know how they knew that my birthday was practically upon me. But there it was, friends and strangers alike, singing at the top of their voices. I took out the cowboy candle, placed it into an envelope, and still have it to remember, when I look at my bookshelves where it is now placed, how a stranger went to Denver and came away with friends.

It was growing cold the morning I left Denver. There was talk of snowstorms in the East. I bought chains for the tires. There was little snow in the streets. It was 7:15 in the morning when I had breakfast; 7:15 and a group of businessmen were discussing the fate of their employees over breakfast at a nearby table. Should they let this one go? What recommended him for further employment with the company? Should they bring in the guy—the guy—Mike, what the hell's his name? Jewish name? Yeah, that's it. Okay. What kind of Christmas bonus? Two hundred? Two-fifty? All the while there was the clatter of cups and saucers, the rattle of silverware on thick Iroquois china. I snatched a look at the circle of sleep-filled faces. Agreed, two-seventy-five bonus. I felt sorry for the men under discussion. I would not like to have my fate decided that early in the morning; it is too close to the time people are executed by firing squads or hanged by the neck until dead. Sleep still clings; the stomach growls for food; the body has not become used to the rhythm of the day; the mind is sluggish, and perhaps the liver too; and the day seems infinitely and impossibly long.

For a Negro the face of the enemy is varied—all sizes and shapes and colors, even black. Often there is no face at all, but an attitude, one that I began to encounter after I had gone north through Cheyenne, where stack upon stack of rusted cars piled high on either side of the road seemed like the gates of ancient cities, and where I saw a youth crossing the street garbed in a ten-gallon hat, cowboy boots, and a continental suit. East of the Warren, Wyoming, missile site, the land becomes a long silent plain with tall, dull-green grasses bending in the wind as waves of the sea. The towns along the way are small and filled with a chill. It was in this region that whenever I presented my credit card at motels and gas stations, I began to encounter suspicion and deep distrust. After I handed them the card, their expressions changed; I no longer was a faceless black. Their eyes came up and saw me for the first time. Often they fingered the precious bit of plastic and gave themselves time to trigger all the ugly hidden machinery that told them that, by everything they knew, I should not have it in my possession. But it *was* in my possession; that was a fact as hard as the card itself, an indisputable fact.

One attendant, his face falling as I handed him the card, rushed into his office. I followed him and watched while he peered at the lost, stolen, or canceled list.

"You won't find my name on there," I assured him.

"I'm supposed to look anyway," he said, and while this was perhaps true, I knew—and he knew—that he didn't make it a practice unless he thought he had a sure thing.

This attitude persists in many places: a Negro isn't supposed to have anything; if he has, he is a thief. Still, the very clerks and attendants who hold this attitude, expect a Negro to have a bundle of cash to pay the bills for cross-country travel. Paradox.

The middle of America is a lonely place; oases of life are few and far between, and usually small and cautious of strangers. The only response I got was coldness. Once in a while, standing outside the car while it was being gassed, I would see the attendants peeping at me, sizing me up. Their eyes would run the length of the car, linger on the guns, slide back to my face and then back to the gas nozzle.

I stumbled on a newly opened stretch of highway in Nebraska. There were only two or three other cars on it. I opened up the car and it galloped. The sun was behind me and it threw ahead the shadow of the car; humped and foreshortened, the gray image sped over the ground, always eight feet before me. The engine gave off a low, steady hum. The landscape, almost bare with winter, flashed by, and where there was green, browned by winter, the sun shone bronze. The land was level, unexciting, and I raced on, calculating the distance and feeling as one with the car. And when at dusk I reached the end of the new highway and joined another, a fleeting confusion and anger assailed me. That could not have been the end of it; there had to be more, more! But there was no more and I had to get in step with the mortals and tread the everyday highways once more.

Strangely, while tearing along that road at great speeds, I thought of New York and missed the trumpet and saxophone players on the subways, the jackleg preachers, the psychotics, the popcorn-caramel stink of the 14th Street subway stop.

IN MEMORY OF J.F.K.
UNITE
FORGET TO HATE

The sign was posted near a restaurant in Savannah, Missouri. Do they mean it, I wondered, flashing past in the grip of swiftly moving traffic en route to Kansas City, Missouri.

As usual, I entered the network of city speedways and chose an exit at random. And, as usual, I found myself very near my hotel. Sometimes I have a great deal of luck, and at others, none.

While waiting to register, an old-maid clerk nudged another, and looking straight at me, said, "Something stinks." The other turned and grimly shook her head. I ignored them both. By now I was a little weary of being the catalyst for white people to make fools of themselves.

But my weariness did not, could not, persist with Thorpe Menn in town. He is the book editor of the Kansas City *Star.* Three brief meetings in New York, a few hours spent listening to jazz in the Vanguard, and we were friends. I am always amazed, when I look back on the beginnings of friendships, as to what made them take. He met me at the hotel, we had drinks and he went into action, calling and gathering people for me to talk with—and for me to talk to—not as a traveler, but as a writer. Thorpe believes I have something important to say and will not believe me when I tell him I haven't. I suppose I think of him with his coat on, scarf dangling wildly and cracking a great big smile. Also, he wears his hat at a rakish angle, which means that he meets life easily, with a good deal of confidence.

The beautiful thing about ugly Kansas City was the people I met through Thorpe. They were all outgoing, determined, intelligent persons—and of all races, colors, and creeds. Of course, I moved in a closed circle, more so because most of them were connected with the Panel of Americans. This organization consists of women who journey to the hinterlands with their message of a united America, but more than that, they seem to live up to their code.

They gathered one night, with their husbands and children, at a party at which I was the guest of honor. Talk ran the length and breadth of the room for a couple of hours, and then Thorpe called them together to listen to what I had to say.

"I've nothing to say," I said. People were gathering near my chair, crouching down on the floor, waiting. I panicked and went to the bathroom, but when I came out they were still there. I am a writer, not a leader and not a man of great wisdom; otherwise, I am sure, my life would have been entirely different. They waited and would not let me out of it; they were gentle with me, as if understanding that I was uneasy. It is a phenomenon of our time; it is seldom good enough for a writer to write; he must also talk, and the more willing he is, the more audiences he will find. As for myself, I prefer to leave the talking to those who enjoy it. I don't.

But, wasn't it something to see them all there? The house must have been bulging. The white neighbors of the white family had become used to such meetings and had set down Esther and Paul Brown as nuts, having so many strange people always coming to their home. The women assured me that when I left, I would have home-cooked ham and cake to take with me, and wouldn't I eat some more right now?

I had known few people in Kansas City ten years earlier and had been uneasy there in the middle of a blistering summer. But now it was cold, and wherever I turned, there was warmth.

Even in the cafeteria of the University of Kansas, where I went with a friend to visit one of his students attending on the Special Scholarship Program, which gives kids from economically and socially deprived backgrounds a chance to go to college. The university sits on a slight, dun-colored bluff and peers down into Lawrence. The co-eds there come sturdy and big-legged, none of that East or West Coast unviolated look, none of that cooling, sometimes antiseptic thinness. The buildings were cut from tough, yellow limestone and looked aged. I left a valuable lighter in the cafeteria, and when, discovering its loss two hours later, I rushed back, it had been turned in. I got to liking that place, at once.

Thorpe is a thoroughgoing jazz buff, an unreconstructed Charlie Parker man, and it was natural that we would go to the Horseshoe to hear the talented singer Bettye Miller, who also plays the piano, and bassist Milt Abel, who also sings. We sat through two sets, and would have stayed for the third, except that there was none—we had missed the first. Even there, I found warmth. Not of the bottle, but of Milt and Bettye. Between sets we talked, and when they were on, they played to me. It goes without saying, except humbly and boastfully at the same time, that I felt good being in Kansas City.

Only the night before I left did a slight chill begin to descend. I had discovered that the Missouri Peace Officers Association would be holding a meeting the next day. The topic was "Civil Disobedience—A Problem for Law Enforcement."

Christmas lights and shopping had no effect on me. I moved on eastward to St. Louis with an increasing depression. I was very tired and had had a bad experience checking out of the hotel. It had been worse than when I checked in. Moreover, traveling in Missouri is rather like traveling in some places in the South. The people I met in Kansas City told me that I had to pick my spots for stopping. There were places where the Panel of Americans hadn't yet been, places where, if you asked for Russian dressing on a corned beef sandwich, they thought you a Communist.

I had last been in St. Louis during a hot summer, when its stink hung thick in the air. I had had to drive around and around looking for the colored YMCA. I did not look for a Y this time, but drove directly to a bold, multicolored structure, up a sleek ramp and then to my room, which was knee-deep luxury. There had not been a single sour look, only curious ones from the Negro parking-lot attendants.

It was my birthday, and I was in St. Louis. It would have been a sorrowful occasion, had I not been able to spend it with two lovely young white women over *coq au vin* and candlelight. I had wearied by now of news of pickets and demonstrations, of accusations that CORE's white members were too militant, that police had clubbed so many people. I really didn't give much of a damn about the presence of the John Birch Society in town. Enough was enough.

My hostesses talked about men, affairs, and divorces. Two lovely young women sitting in the cold of a St. Louis night, the fog dripping heavily outside, talking about what seemed elusive to them. Or perhaps they were fooling themselves. I looked at the flickering candles and thought of the women in New York, the roommates who also served *coq au vin* by candlelight, talked about the arts, superficially about civil rights—and men.

The prettier girl was from the Deep South, but had been away so long that she had no accent. But I found myself retreating from her words, her smile, the flashes of light sent fleeing from her brunette hair. I didn't trust her. The other was also a brunette and came from a nearby town. I had met her in a New York publicity agency.

In such a situation one can become aware, what with the drinks before dinner, the wine in the food, and the wine at dinner, of a sense of waiting for something to happen. The right combination of words, the right tone of voice, the right look of the eye at the right time. Who's to begin the game? Who's to leave and go to a movie and who's to stay? One went out for cigarettes and returned; the other cleared the table and stayed in the kitchen for a little while. Time enough with both to have said the words, had the words been wanted, had it been right to say them. I didn't really know, past sensing, and I was too tired really to care.

The candles burned lower; the wine was gone. As if reminding me that it was my birthday, speeding, tiny hurts had begun to race through my body, teeth, head, legs, arms, chest. One more Scotch—for the sneaking little reminders that I could now look forward to creeping old age and short breath. Zest—had it gone with the dinner, the conversation that echoed all others, the women sitting and talking, twirling the ends of their hair as if waiting for a *deus ex machina* to rescue them from their candle-lit lethargy?

Peggy walked to the door with me and out to the landing. She was the one who had fled New York. I could see a man waiting for a bus down on the street. His pale face glowed through the dark and fog. I did not know if Peggy saw him. We embraced and kissed, as we had when I arrived, a friendly kiss recalling a couple of dinners and a night of listening to Ornette Coleman with his new sound when it was new.

The face of the man in the street had frozen in our direction. I still did not know if Peggy had seen him—or had she seen him first? Distrust is like a worm that must destroy the entire apple, from the inside out. If she saw him, didn't she care that she had to live here? Didn't she know what he was capable of doing? This was Missouri. I have been set upon in New York for less. Or was it that she thought that any result of our embrace would only affect me.

On the whole the white American male is a peculiar creature. He tends to have a proprietary interest in any white female seen with a Negro male. He doesn't have to know the woman at all. In such a situation he can rise to scowling, insulting heights of incredible chivalry. If he is alone. Put him with two of his fellows and he is primed to begin a race riot—over something not his concern at all. Well, we would see.

I went downstairs and crossed the street to where the man stood. I passed in front of him, expectantly. Ready? I was ready. A sick kind of joy welled up in me. Parts of a hundred scattered dreams came together in a completed puzzle. Only when I had passed him did I fully realize that my right arm was tense, my fist drawn so hard that the knuckles ached. No wonder, I thought, getting into the car, my right armpit perspired more than my left; it had been that way since New England.

I didn't linger long in Indianapolis, a city that in my estimation ranks high on the list of ugly American cities. As I was passing through, I heard a newscaster refer to Fidel Castro as a "bad, bearded big mouth," a series of words that did not consist of any news whatsoever, but an opinion, propaganda. In the face of all the slanted news and propaganda, it is the exceptional person who edits his own ideas from those of the newscasters. I am both startled and frightened when I hear people using phrases they have come to think their own when talking about politics or commercial items. During the time I worked in the research department of an advertising agency, I came to know that the success of an advertising campaign is largely based on how many key words or phrases in the "message" were repeated back by voice or in writing.

Winter exposes the cities and towns of America. It is not because the landscape that holds them is stark, it is rather the overwhelming sense that everyone is hibernating one gets passing through the country. Even the holidays brought them little cheer. Only an irritating movement, as if by hook or crook the ritual must be maintained.

I found it so in Chicago, now held fast in the grip of a bitter lakeside winter. Sullen, child-slapping people moved angrily along the aisles of Christmas-decorated stores; long lines waited for Santa Claus. The foxy girls of a couple of months before were evil with the bitter cold. Even so, pickets manned the Loop protesting the school de facto segregation and opposing the buying of Christmas presents from white stores. But for me it remained an island of rest. Friends served up a chitlin dinner and I plunged in as though I hadn't had them in years. Chitlins were a medieval food in Europe and came to the American South via the French settlers. Once classed as "nigger food" and all but given away at hog-killing time, they are now frozen or canned and sold at fairly high prices.

As usual, Doc Hasbrouck and I talked endlessly about America, about Syracuse. We went through his library for Tocqueville, Krause, Lerner, Paine, Jefferson; for Mills, Du Bois, Olmstead, Dollard.

We sat and drank, two eyeglassed, pajama-clad souls trying to find something solid. And then, as if to mock our efforts to find out where we stood in America, we watched a television show, "1776." We didn't see Crispus Attucks, a colored man said to be the first to die in the American Revolution, nor did we hear any mention of Peter Salem or the others.

Doc looked over and gave me a cynical smile. "Man, if you aren't in at the beginning, where you *were*, you've missed the damn train; and we're still trying to catch up with it."

We had reached that moment again, the one we always reach when we talk about America. And it is the moment all Negroes reach in their search. You know the moment by the sudden falling away of conversation; the bewilderment and anger, the helplessness, boil down to a four-letter word. In the very next hour, however, a Negro will say: "Okay, but I can't think of another place in the world where I'd like to leave my passport." So, you are compelled to start searching all over again.

The night before I left Doc's I dreamed this dream: I was driving. The car started to rise on the rear wheels, taking off at a 45-degree angle. Suddenly it flipped over and I was under it, being crushed. I cursed and gave a violent kick, throwing the covers to the floor. I woke up. I looked out. More snow. I packed slowly, more depressed than ever. Once we dreamed of floods and earthquakes, locusts and plagues, all within the human experience and grist for the mind. Now we dream of collision, jumping from skyscrapers or sinking on luxury liners. Tomorrow it will be hanging out in space, rocket fuel gone, or entering a magnetic field and becoming lost in a galaxy.

The great, gray-black Gary steel mills plowed endless clouds of smoke into the dark snow-spewing sky. I drove dully, the seat belt tight against my waist. I had driven through thirty-eight states so far, and had covered close to 15,000 miles. With few exceptions, I had slept in a different bed almost every night. The smell of motels and hotels hung all about me: the soap, the deodorized baths, the food, the rugs, the mattresses.

Now I was cutting across Ohio instead of going down. In mid-afternoon I saw a patrol car in front of me. I checked the speedometer, and it read seventy, the limit. I held steady for about ten miles. The cop pulled into a crossover. I maintained the same speed. Farther along I saw coming up behind me what I thought was another patrol car. I made room for it to pass. But at the moment it should have passed, it didn't and I glanced around to find the car keeping pace with me. The officer signaled me to pull over.

After Kentucky, I had been followed by police or troopers in Georgia, Tennessee, Mississippi; I had been pulled over in Illinois and California. Followed, pulled over, and made to know that I was a lone black man in a big car, and vulnerable as hell. I had had enough. I snatched off the seat belt and rolled down the window. It didn't give me room enough and I kicked open the door.

"What's the matter?" I shouted at the trooper. He didn't answer as he walked to the car. And then I decided to commit it all—my body, if he wanted it—for I could not take any more harassment.

"Let's see your license," he said.

"I asked you what the trouble was." That was not what he wanted. The ritual says that I must hand it over to him without a word.

"I want to see your license."

I gave it to him, smelling the odor of a man about to exercise the "insolence of office." If I'd been over the limit, he would have said so and ticketed me. It was the old game, "You black, me white, and I'm a cop too." Some white people believe they are the only ones who know that game.

He fingered the license and then, leaning casually in the window, said, "John, what's your occupation?"

I laughed. What does occupation have to do with an alleged traffic violation? Was it supposed to tell him that I had money enough to pay him off? Was it to let him know that I was the "right" kind of Negro, the one with political connections that could make it hot for him? Was I supposed to be jobless and transporting drugs, a corpse, or girls across the state line? Police and troopers of America, on a slow day you can always find a Negro or two wandering through your state. Brighten up that day by making like exactly what you are.

"My name," I shouted, "is Mr. Williams." I'm sure that cops and troopers use the familiar with many white people, but this one I smelled out. "John" was synonymous with "boy." He snatched his arm from the window. I flung my authorization for the trip at him. I watched him as he read it, and thought: Not only am I not the "right" kind of Negro, not only will I not pay you off, but I am about five seconds away from total commitment, which means five seconds off your ass.

He glanced over the top of the sheet. "Mr. Williams, you were doing eighty coming down the road. I was in front and pulled off. When I caught up with you, you were doing eighty-two."

"You're a liar. I was doing seventy. I didn't know *you* were in front of me, but I saw a patrol car. You turned off and came sneaking back up the pike because you had nothing better to do? Eighty? Take me in and prove it."

"Mr. Williams——"

"Tired of taking all this crap from you guys."

"Mr. Williams——"

"You're going to run this nonsense *and* yourselves right into the ground."

Cars were slowing up as they passed us. The trooper's face took on an anxious look. Yes, I was rambling in my anger, but I was ready to go. What is more, for the insults I delivered, he would have taken me in *had he been right*. Instead, he returned to his car and I drove on at seventy miles an hour.

The explosion of anger, pent up for so many weeks, left me more exhausted than ever. But I kept thinking about it: the direct or indirect insults of clerks, bellboys, attendants, cops, strangers in passing cars. I believe the white friends I made on the trip would have been just as incensed, just as knowing. But they were far from me and I was completely vulnerable to a long series of attacks against my black person. A physical attack would have been better; I never know just how effective my words are, or even if they are understood.

Like Chicago, Cleveland rests on a lake and curls around its shore. I never think of it as big, and yet, it isn't small. I became sick there and had to stay until I felt better. I was a stranger and so did not know which route to take into the city to avoid being dragged from the car and beaten to a pulp. I was lucky. It was night when I came through the Italian section, and had the fortune of a fool. I did not find out about the boiling racial antipathies until I was stretched on my bed, a heating pad lying gingerly upon my aching belly. Then I was feeling too ill to care.

One night there was a news flash over the radio. The Baldwin Hills section of Los Angeles had been inundated by waters from a nearby reservoir that had burst without warning. Since my folks lived not far away, I placed a call. The phones were out of order. All right. I would try again in another half hour, and if there were still no answer, I'd call my brother or sister, who live some distance away from my parents. The line was open the second time and Ola answered. "See there, they didn't want us in, now look what's happened to them." My parents were all right; the waters had gone the other way, north.

I went back to bed and nursed my belly, hoping to be able to see the Karamu House production of Lorraine Hansberry's play, *A Raisin in the Sun*. The first time I saw it in New York, with Claudia McNeil, Sidney Poitier, and Ruby Dee, I rushed out of the theater at the conclusion; I had ridden through each act on a purely emotional level; there had been something of Ola and me there. I had taken it very badly, for days. The Karamu production was only an echo of the New York production, but it was still very moving, although I had thought a great deal about the play, and read it, and knew it now on an altogether different level. Most of the audience was white, a fact that sent the Negroes with me into grumbles. Why didn't Negroes support their own theater? That old, stale question. The majority of white people don't support "their" theater either.

What I remember most vividly about Cleveland was a day spent in the Christmas-shopping rush at Higbee's Department Store. I had recovered enough to stand it. On the way to the store I stopped to have the car washed at a garage along the lakefront. The wind came yowling and leaping from the water bringing with it bitter, bitter cold. The car wash was manned by the roughest, toughest bunch of Negroes I've ever seen. I tried to start a conversation with one, and he cut his eyes at me as if to say, "Aw man, why the hell don't you shut up?" They were so tough that I didn't know whether they were going to return the car to me or not. I don't know that I would have had nerve enough to ask. But they did release it and I was so grateful that I'm sure I overtipped. It was worth it.

The department store had a section set aside for the "Little Shoppers" called Twigbee's. Fine, I thought. I hung around and watched the parents bring their eager children to the entrance. There the children signed slips stating how much money they wanted to spend (the parents were very positive about that) and on whom. But once they were inside, the guides at the entrance vanished. The kids went haywire while their parents, set outside by high walls and unable to see except through a few portholes, waited nervously. When the kids arrived at the exit cashiers, set up on line like a supermarket, they had overspent. The tough parents made them take the extra items back; the soft ones cursed Twigbee's and Higbee's and paid. It was the worst example of Christmas huckstering I've ever witnessed. For many parents, when their kids finished there, Christmas was a souring thing.

On Route Eight, south from Cleveland, there was a large sign that read:

WHY IMPEACH EARL WARREN?
AMERICANS FOR CONSTITUTIONAL GOVERNMENT

It was a much bigger sign than the one I had seen outside Kansas City, the one calling on people to forget hate, more prominent and, undoubtedly, cost more to put up.

My dream almost came true in western New York State. To begin with, the roads were sheets of ice, and then a blizzard came. I joined a line of cars moving slowly along, half on the road and half off. Later, when the road seemed better, I looked in the mirror and saw a car overtaking me. It was moving slowly, but coming on nevertheless through the deep snow in the passing lane. At the moment it should have passed me, it didn't. The mind automatically measures those seconds. I turned quickly to see the car, driven by a woman, skidding toward me. To avoid her, I went off the road, catching deep snow and gravel, and stopped on the shoulder. The woman's car continued to spin and skid. When it stopped, she was facing me and only a few yards away. I took out my blinker light and walked back up the road in driving snow to warn the oncoming cars. I shouted, asked her if she were all right. She gave an angry jerk of her head, got her car straightened out, and drove off in a huff. She had behaved as if it had been my fault. Had I been in the Rockies or the Midwest, I might have become angry. But I was going to Syracuse; Christmas was but a few days away; and nothing in the world could have made me angry. I was only tired.

Driving through snowstorms on icy roads for long distances is a most nerve-racking experience. It is a paradox that the snow, coming down gently, blowing gleefully in a high wind, all the while lays down a treacherous carpet, freezes the windows, blocks the view. The might of automated man is muted. The horses, the powerful electrical systems, the deep-tread tires, all go for nothing. One minute the road feels firm, and the next the driver is sliding over it, light as a feather, in a panic, wondering what the heavy trailer trucks coming up from the rear are going to do. The trucks are like giants when you have to pass them, not at sixty or seventy as you do when the road is dry, but at twenty-five and thirty. Then their engines sound unnaturally loud. Snow, slush and chips of ice spray from beneath the wheels, obscure the windshield, and rattle off your car. Beneath the wheels there is plenty of room for you to skid and get mashed to a pulp. Inch by inch you move up, past the rear wheels, the center wheels, the cab, the front wheels, all sliding too slowly by. Straight ahead you continue, for to cut over sharply would send you into a skid, right in front of the vehicle. At last, there is distance enough, and you creep back over, in front of the truck now, but with the sound of its engine still thundering in your ears.

I arrived in Syracuse in a muddy brown dark. There were traffic snarls from one end of the city to the other. It was quitting time, and those who had left the factories and the offices were shopping. I crept and slid crosstown in deep, gray-brown snow, and pulled up in the driveway, clutching a bottle of brandy, and leaped out. The snow was knee deep.

"Well, look who's here," Greg said. "It's the old man."

"Hi, old man," Dennis said. We shook hands all around.

We don't kiss anymore, even on the cheek. Then we sat looking at each other.

"A glass," I said. They watched me drink and exchanged smiles. I've taught them how to mix pretty good Martinis for me. Their mother arrived and we sat down to dinner, and then she and I drank the brandy. There was mail, and I went through that. There was not much else that night. The return had been quiet; there had been no questions. All the warm things had been cloaked.

"We waited until you got here to help put up the tree."

"You look tired. Have another drink, Dad."

"How long are you here for this time?"

I left and drove through the snow-filled streets to my aunt's home; that is where I stay on my visits there. She wasn't home and I let myself in, unloaded the car. Her son, my cousin, lives upstairs with his family in that building, the last apartment house in the block. Local businesses are spreading from the center of the town outward and old houses are being torn down. When I was young the Rescue Mission was next door and a series of red-brick homes, with green steps and porches, ranged down the street. A blacksmith had a shop in a rear alley. The Savoy Hotel, which used to be a haven for Negro waiters, porters, and musicians, is across the street, as decayed and decrepit as it was when I first knew it. No Negro traveler has to go there now. East Washington Street used to be the main thoroughfare for Negroes twenty years ago, and then, added to it, was South Townsend Street. Both are now quiet and tranquil; the houses have been bulldozed out. New highways and Urban Renewal. Once you knew everyone in the city and where he lived. Now it is impossible to know all the Negroes or in which part of town they reside.

That is one way to measure change. Another was to go upstairs and congratulate my cousin on his brand new political career; he had been elected supervisor of the fifteenth ward, the first black Republican to gain the post in 194 years of black existence in Syracuse.

I was very tired when I returned downstairs. My aunt wasn't in town. I showered, fixed up my bed, and got in it, but sleep wouldn't come. A sheath of light lanced downward past the window, and I could see snow falling silently, thickly. I had gone through hundreds of cities and towns, had traversed six mountain ranges while living out of a suitcase. I should have fallen right off to sleep. But in a way I was home and it was time for a preliminary summing up.

I was remembering now the kind of caution people of position exuded when I saw them, and how many of them had ended brief discussions by saying "Don't quote me," or "I wouldn't like for this to leave the room, all right?" I remembered the professor at Alabama State. How fearful people are to speak on almost anything pertaining to our lives today. Freedom of speech is still with us, but freedom from retaliation after speaking freely is not.

Upstairs, one of the kids started crying. I glanced at my watch. It was late and all I had done was lie awake and smoke and watch the snow come down.

Another cigarette. I felt I had been permitted a rare chance to see America and to meet its people again. My view, moving through the country, exposing my entire being to its moods and whims, was that there is a great emptiness, a stalking thing, sad and frightening at once. Politics, through which we come to have government, has been seen by Americans, I believe, to be an empty thing because they too seldom have an actual part in it. And if the science of politics has little meaning, can government? This nation offers every single person a chance to participate in government, but at the same time denies them that opportunity. Thus, the average man who is concerned with the nation beyond the affairs of his family, town, and self is hard put to find the handle to help change things for the better. The late President Kennedy better should have suggested *ways* and *means* for people to involve themselves in their country than to merely ask them to do so. How does one begin?

A sense of change does lay hard upon the land, but few of us seem to understand the processes of it, or more important, how to adapt to it. I felt very often that across the ranges and plains of this land there was a growing feeling that government does not have as much power as we have been led to believe. And if central power no longer lies in government, where does it lie, and why, if it is a benevolent power, does it remain hidden?

The murder of John F. Kennedy heightened the sense of alienation from government. During the first week of mourning, people seemed to attach great hope to the possibility that something they could touch and feel beyond the grief over his death would emerge. Perhaps the waterfall would back up, the kaleidoscope would stop whirling—but that feeling persisted for no more than seven or eight days.

Morning. The snow had piled up again, sending every citizen back into his private little shell. I heard my cousin, Moon, come pounding down the stairs on his way to work. His car racked and coughed and finally started. Now the busloads of students began to move up toward the university. Trucks and more cars. The city was awake and in motion. I must have sounded very bad when I called New York. I had been out of touch for a month and a half. My friend and agent, Carl Brandt, Jr., said, "What's the matter, you sound like hell?"

I admitted being tired. But I must have sounded worse, for he planned to come up Christmas night and talk with me to find out what was the matter.

Like someone in a daze, I made the rounds of friends. My stomach kicked up again, but I ignored it; Christmas was approaching. I drank and talked and visited some more. I Christmas-shopped with the boys and lunched and dined with them. We plodded through snowdrifts to go to here and there. The tree was up and stacks of presents glittered beneath it. Everywhere there were food and drink, carols, songs, and decorations. I went to a basketball game with Dennis and met an old teacher of mine stalking down the halls of the school which now seemed so small. We sat and watched the game, Dennis on the edge of his chair, muttering under his breath because his team was losing. Red-cheeked, bare-legged cheerleaders, dressed to show off blooming femininity, bounded and shouted and somersaulted, and Dennis grinned approvingly.

One night I crept back to my aunt's house and sat alone listening to *The Messiah,* tippling brandy and feeling lonely in that house I had known practically all my life. It was as much a stranger now as the city and the people I had known. My friends, people I had gone to school with, are somehow self-conscious when I am there. I reflected all I had done was to move away from there. Why should that have raised walls so thick they blocked out the past?

I saw Mayor William F. Walsh one afternoon, I don't know why now, but I knew the trip wasn't over and I thought in the random conversation, there might be something of value, but there wasn't. I used to know Walsh when he was

with the old New York State Commission Against Discrimination. I met him when I filed a case against Lucky
Strike cigarettes.

I had applied for a job through the state employment services and one day I received a call while in class. My first
thought was that my wife had become ill, or Greg. I went
to the phone and was relieved to find that it was only the
job. The section manager was coming by the house to interview me that afternoon, so I had to cut classes.

He came to our apartment, knocked on the door, and when
I opened it, his mouth fell open. He hesitated, and at that
moment I could see that the job was not going to be mine.
My wife and child were in one of the rear rooms and there
were no witnesses to the conversation, in which he said he
couldn't hire me because I was Negro. I took the case to Bill
Walsh, and the determination was "No Cause"—for complaint.

Perhaps I was thinking of that case when I sat across the
desk from Bill now, who was, from everything I heard, a reluctant Republican mayor. Contrary to many people who had
nothing to say, Bill kept saying, "Take this down," or "You'll
want to take this down."

I left him to get into the swing of Christmas Eve. The most
stolid people begin to come alive late afternoon of Christmas Eve; they start feeling "Christmasy" and the sense of
the season comes rushing up to be drowned in booze and
gift-giving, gift-receiving. I was no exception. Christmas was
just about here. The boys walked around the tree counting
their presents. Which would they open before going to bed?

"Not a single one," Greg said vehemently. "I'm waiting
until morning."

"I am too," Dennis said.

On the spot I concocted, through a swirl of Scotches and
water, a new set of lyrics for *Hark! the Herald Angels Sing,*
and, while Dennis blew on his trumpet, I sang:

> "Hark the drunken angels sing,
> Bring more wine and everything,
> Bourbon, Scotch, and cognac too,
> Apple cobbler and turkey stew."

Greg refused to join us in such a wild display of sacrilegious-
ness. He stoppered his ears. My ex-wife, a tolerant soul, put

up with us; her mother shook her head; she knew it all the time, that I was an irreligious nut. Fittingly, there was more snow blotting out the multitude of Christmas lights on display in the houses along the street. And so, Christmas came.

It was a quiet day, with all the polite things said upon the opening of the gifts. There were few surprises; the boys got just what they wanted. There were visitors who came, briefly, remembering the old days, but overlaying them with laughter, jokes, a galloping heartiness. Brandt came late in the afternoon, and the boys and I picked him up at his hotel, then Brandt and I dropped them off and went to dinner at a restaurant that seemed sad because it was not crowded. And we talked. He had brought with him a gift from C. D. B. Bryan, a fellow writer, a turtleneck dickey, to cheer me up. Christmas night came and we parted; the next morning I would continue on to New York and he to Vermont. The trip was not yet completed.

The only adjective that comes to mind when I think of New York City is mighty. It seemed that I had been away from it for a hundred years, but a day's hunting trip, only 100 miles away, makes me feel like that. New York, in a very real way, is not America. Beyond the Hudson toward which the afternoon sun was slanting, another land existed. New York can only be placed in the same category as London, Paris, or Rome. The people in those metropolitan centers are vastly different from those who live outside them.

Hustling along, I took a wrong turn north of the city, trying to find Bruckner Boulevard. I turned down a street, irritated at the delay—I could see the Empire State Building clearly, and it made me anxious to get into the city— and heard a long, sharp whistle. I looked around and saw a woman signaling me. "Hey, mister. You're going the wrong way on a one-way street." She gave directions and I continued on downtown, picked my way through the traffic, and finally arrived at the Albert Hotel, an establishment that defies description, for it is not merely a hotel, but an apartment house that caters to all kinds of people. And wherever I traveled I always met someone who has stayed at the Albert, with its one working elevator and aged bellman. The charm of the Albert is its location, almost in the heart of Greenwich Village.

New York must be the fastest changing city in the world,

except the ones the Israelis are throwing up every hour on the edge of the Negev. My barber had moved; my street was now one-way going north. A cafeteria had been opened in a new building that had been but a vacant lot when I left. An old cafeteria on the corner of Broadway and 8th Street had come down. I had survived many months on the 90-cent specials that place offered, and it seemed that some part of my past had been completely obliterated. Further down, a whole block was being leveled. Change: constant, brutal, bewildering.

The rich and the poor are being crushed closer and closer together in New York, but the differences, at least between whites, are not as obvious as they are between poor blacks and rich whites.

I returned to a New York that in only a few months had done a surprising job of "integrating" television, commercials and otherwise. It was done so quickly and easily that I wondered what had held it back. I knew very well what had accomplished the change: the violent summer of 1963. And New York hadn't let up on its underground campaign in a variety of public-impact businesses to "Get a Negro!"

As could have easily been predicted, plays about Negroes peppered the off-Broadway boards. Genet's *The Blacks* was *still* running; Langston Hughes' *Trumpets of the Lord* was playing; *In White America* was drawing overflow crowds, and solid, sober notices. I saw it and liked it. The confrontations of Negro leaders with Presidents Andrew Johnson and Woodrow Wilson were bitter indeed to watch. Our Presidents have come a long way. Since the play is based on Negro history, with which many Negroes (not all) are familiar, I would recommend it to white people if it lasts or is ever staged again. I had expected to see James Baldwin's *Blues for Mr. Charlie* and Lorraine Hansberry's *The Sign in Sidney Brustein's Window*. Neither was running and I had to console myself with J. P. Donleavy's adaptation of his own novel, *The Ginger Man*. It was not a consoling time, but one of high elation and superb performances. I think it has to be true that, when an author sees life on this earth as it is, it is often very hard for critics to swallow, and they pan the work. Such was the case with Donleavy's play. As the novelist Chester Himes would say, "I liked the very hell out of it."

That is something New York has in overflowing amounts,

authors and critics, both coming hell-for-leather from opposite ends down the same track. Sometimes they accomplish a physical impossibility; they occupy the same place at the same time. That is, the critic agrees with the author. More often, however, the immutable law of physics holds sway—and there is a collision.

The *Mirror,* as predicted, had checked into oblivion. The New York papers had never recovered from the strike of 1963, which lasted from January until March and killed off a number of books, including one of mine.

Death had claimed a number of people: Edith Piaf, Jean Cocteau, Dinah Washington, Aldous Huxley, Paul Hindemith, and my friend of only two years, A. J. Liebling.

Between Christmas and New Year's, office and private parties rage unchecked in New York. Romances bloom or are broken, as are marriages. One drinks too much and/or talks too much. People are determined to "stay home this year," and in order not to stay home alone, they begin working on their New Year's Eve guest lists right after Thanksgiving. Partying seems a way of life and it is with no little relief that the holiday season passes into dreary January with its flood of white sales. The check of the calendar begins: 1964, someone said, had all the holidays on a Saturday.

Going down the dim stairway in the Albert one day, I met a clean-cut white Southern young man. He held a slim attaché case and a leather-handled umbrella. He wore glasses and was dressed immaculately.

"Excuse me," he said as I was passing, "do you get to New York very often?"

"I live here," I said, put off by his accent.

"Then you know where things are going on."

"What kind of things?"

"Anything and everything," he said boldly, and I had to laugh. I'll bet "anything and everything." What, was he one of those nuts out of Southern literature? Had I passed him in the South and asked for directions he would not have looked at me twice. That type. But now, black and a New Yorker, as knowing as all New Yorkers are supposed to be, he was but a second from baring a soul to me which must have been ugly. I shrugged. I had no idea what he was interested in, boys, girls, or both; maybe he was looking for a "Mammy-whipping." "Try MacDougal Street," I said. It is the place where I send all the strangers who stop me, thinking I know where the good things are.

It is a street that in the summer reeks of pizza and hot dogs and sauerkraut. Gape-doored coffeehouses line the street; homosexual men and women line the iron rails of Washington Square Park. Tourists, thousands of them, drift through. The hipsters, sharpies, and beatniks man the corners looking for the "live ones" like my young Southern gentlemen. They are the boys who can turn up "anything and everything" and a bit more.

"Thank you, my friend," the Southerner said and skipped on his way.

"Any time, buddy."

It is a strange thing, but people really get friendly whenever there is a snowstorm in New York and they have to walk in the freshly cleared streets. But the snowstorm that came prevented my going to Washington by car. Planes already in the air were being diverted to other cities; the train was the only transportation left. The evening before I had had dinner with Richard Yates, another novelist and former speech writer for Attorney General Robert Kennedy. He had planned to drive down with me; now that was impossible. I called and asked him to meet me at Penn Station. But when I went out, I knew I would have to move the car, and if I moved it, I might just as well park it somewhere near Penn. Accordingly I picked Dick up and we took the train.

There is a chummy way to travel, by train. Slow and easy, irritatingly slow, the landscape drifting backward at a snail's pace. The louder the voices were, the less prominent positions the passengers held in government, I concluded, for the train was filled with people who "looked like they belonged in Washington."

I met Dick at Bread Loaf the same year I met John Engels. Dick, in fact, had returned two seasons as a member of the faculty. Our conversations were fluttering things, up and running one moment and flopping the next so we could exchange papers, the *Times* and the *Herald Tribune*.

Then it was time for lunch and we moved to the diner, thirsty for the Martinis first. I sat in the diner, next to the window, and lazily watched the aged, bumbling waiters move through the jammed aisle. I had not been to Washington by train since 1946 when my cousin and I went to

Georgia, ostensibly to get an education, but really to play football. At that time we had to wait until almost all the white diners were finished and then, with great courtesy, we were shown to the Jim Crow corner and the thick green curtain was pulled, closing off the view of us, which might have been distressing to white people. There was no green curtain now, but you don't forget the past just because it is the past.

Baltimore, and memories of Billie Holiday, and then Washington, where the minions of government huddled before the station, furiously hailing cabs. I remembered that spot too, for Moon and I had arrived there at night and the lights had been shining on the Capitol dome. An elderly Negro woman who had been waiting for a cab finally became angry and began shouting at the taxi starter. Cabs had not been integrated in 1946; nothing in Washington had been. The woman became so loud and furious silhouetted in the light of the dome that we believed the starter would hit her. If he had, we would have had to step in; there was no other choice. We stood and listened and watched and sweated. When the crisis reached the point of no return, a Negro cab driver drove up and took her away. Moon's relief and mine was immeasurable.

But Washington this time struck me as having no little amount of charm. We secured a cab without trouble and went to Dick's apartment; I had canceled my reservation at a motor hotel.

I suppose that in some circles Mrs. Jane McClary would be considered a socialite. I don't know. We arranged to meet not far from the White House, where she was working. She, she said over the phone, would be wearing a green scarf. I would be wearing a beard. We had very little trouble finding each other in the little French restaurant, the Chez Françoise. There seemed to be a variety of people there from all over the world: Africans, Chinese, and of course, the French. An acquaintance of Mrs. John F. Kennedy, Mrs. McClary had volunteered to work on the mail, which was still coming in in piles, extending sympathy. At the moment, they were still processing it, nation by nation. And an entire auditorium had been given over to the toys sent to the Kennedy children. Mrs. McClary traveled eighty miles from Virginia, round trip each day, to help out. Very active in the NAACP in her small community, she urged me to come down and visit a meeting scheduled the next day, but I could not go. Distance, sometimes, is very necessary to see the whole clearly.

It happened once more. Mrs. McClary told me when she first arrived that there was a great deal of work to do and that she had to hurry back to work. And I had planned some things. But, the more we talked, the more important the ideas we both had became and lunch ran late. When it was over, and the ill-attended parade for visiting Italian President Segni had broken up, we agreed to meet that night at the home of the columnist and analyst Marquis Childs.

I returned to Dick's and tore him away from his typewriter. What, I wanted to know, was Washington like when Kennedy had been alive?

"Government was fun, kind of," he said. "Now it isn't."

As a result, a lot of people were leaving Washington. The fun, drive, glamour, and intelligence were fleeing; Washington seemed to be settling itself for austerity, scandal, and drastic change. We talked on as the late afternoon shadows crept into the room. Washington was like Hollywood in a way, only its personalities were political figures. And they sometimes put on remarkable performances.

Marquis Childs' photo on his syndicated columns show him as a half-smiling, reticent person. He is, in fact, quite stocky and there is nothing reticent about him. The company was stellar; there was even a tuxedo or two, an ambassador and his wife, and NBC's Richard Harkness, and Brandon of the London *Times,* to whom I said, "You gave us the Industrial Revolution and now we've become almost overwhelmed by automation."

"And so are we. That is your gift to us," he answered.

Out of a flurry of conversation in which Mark Childs was engaged, I heard him say angrily, "The Bobby Baker case is only a cover-up for the TFX controversy." I had forgotten about the Baker case on the road, but it was still very much alive in Washington.

"Warren doesn't see any use in going further on the Oswald thing," another man said.

And still another in yet another group, "It's RFK on the second spot for the Dems. It won't be Barry for the GOP, though. He's an absolute ass."

One could not help feeling that he had been invited to a

special session of a special club, for here were people close to everything who hour by hour were deluged by rumor and fact and had to separate the two; the people who knew Presidents and would-be Presidents, and who could help make or break them. An easy sense of power was there, and the grace with which the powerful often move. Yet, the issues of importance did not seem to be there; rather the issues of the moment and those, sometimes unfortunately, are what newsmen must deal with.

That night and the others sped by. Washington had a soft look because of the snow and there was even something exciting about trying to catch a cab late at night, or getting a car out of a snowdrift or listening to the merry clinking of car chains.

There were dinners in quiet, plush restaurants in which sleek diplomats sat talking in corners, twirling cognac in great snifters. The Goldwater signs were up; one of the largest hung on the front of the Duryea Building on Connecticut Avenue, and it showed the senator with all the crags and crevices touched out; he looked very benign. I could enjoy Washington night life, from what I saw of it, but the feeling persisted in many places, that it was now the rule to be nicer than possible to Negroes; it was a nagging, uneasy feeling. I could never forget what Washington was when many of the same people lived here. And I could not forget that it was a city my family, on the way up from Mississippi, paused in, briefly, and moved on, for it was too much like home; it was still South. I would be one of the first to admit that it is losing that posture, but then, it had better lose it.

It is an enclave, Washington, bubbling over with more women than men. It is a tight, closed circle that sometimes upon its many revolutions spills out the dangerous or superfluous person. It is a city that enjoys, I think, more historical than factual eminence. And it is not yet gauche, at a New York cocktail party, to casually throw out the names of Washingtonians, "so-and-so's aide" and the like. We are only occasionally reminded that Washington is the only city in America with a Negro majority.

I took my leave of Yates one morning. He was already up and cigarette smoke clung heavily around his desk. Once again I was reminded of how lonely and even ugly is the craft of writing. Yates would be at his desk while the sun galloped overhead. Cars passing outside might bring him the realization that an outside world did indeed exist. Phone calls would do that too, perhaps. But he could not write and share completely the thousands of enticements of the outside. The outside, like the moon, could only exist in phases.

An hour before my appointment with Arthur M. Schlesinger, Jr., then White House Historian, I took a cab to the Washington Monument. The sun was bright, and camera bugs, despite the snow, were out slipping through the narrow, cleared walkways. I had the cabbie drive very slowly around the grounds; I was remembering once again the March on Washington, which had taken place in August, 1963. The grounds were still and cold, sterile, and it was hard to visualize once more the multitudes of people who had gathered there as barons of the American spirit to petition King John on the banks of Runnymede, petitioning not for a new Magna Charta of guaranteed rights, but for the institution of the old.

I had left New York, a passenger in one of two cars filled with black people and white people. Our lunches were packed and sleep had been set aside. When we emerged from the Holland Tunnel and gained the New Jersey Turnpike, hundreds of cars and buses, like ourselves, were hurtling southward, signs snapping in the midnight wind, FREEDOM, or FREEDOM NOW. When we pulled into a Howard Johnson's later, we knew everyone in the parking lot was going to Washington. There were the signs on the cars and buses, and stacks of lunches. Greetings rolled into the night and black hands and white hands together slammed car doors and proceeded on to the capital, some cars filled with waking and crying babies.

The great caravan sped on. We waved as we passed other cars and the people in them waved to us. Snatches of song were strung along the highway. On they came, the cars and buses. Sleep was impossible. The spirit soared at the sight of so many people, and the spine itched with knowing in some ancient, instinctive way that something great and electric was moving at last in the nation. By dawn the buses were already prowling toward their appointed places in the city. The cars were from everywhere, north, south and west. By ten, the folk singers were at work. Their voices drifted down from the speakers set high atop the Washington Monument, now gleaming like a golden bar in the sunlight. Contingents hoisted their signs for everyone to see. Newsmen dashed through the crowds or mounted platforms. Still they came. There were more folk singers, and planes bringing more marchers droned overhead. How many thousands? The people swept from the Mall up to the foot of the shaft, 25,000; 50,000; 100,000. They were everywhere. Odetta sang, Joan Baez, the Chad Mitchell Trio. From all sides they came; they disembarked from their buses and walked down Constitution Avenue, banners and posters held high; from the airport and train stations they came. One man skated in. Finally, they spilled over the mound and down over the Mall, a slowly spreading river.

And suddenly it was time to march, and over a quarter of a million people, black and white, moved down the roads to the Lincoln Memorial. They were so tightly massed that it was impossible to cross between the ranks. Overhead on lifts and mottled with the shadows of millions of leaves from the great trees that lined the streets, the television cameras swung back and forth, peered down into the crowds. The armies shuffled along singing, arm in arm, hand in hand, strangers no more, and it hurt to look into some of the faces: so close, the power of the sun at full shine. Some of the marchers were so old they had to be wheeled, and some were so young they had to be carried, and some so sightless they had to be led. Some people wept as they moved along, and unable to extricate their hands from those of their newfound friends, let the tears roll freely. Some people smiled, but they all moved with the innate grace of those endowed with a powerful purpose. The marchers pinched in from two roads, spilled onto the Mall, back, back, back, until the grass around the Reflection Pool was entirely covered with humanity. And still they came.

I sat on the steps of the Lincoln Memorial with Bob Johnson of *Jet,* and Dick Gregory. We weren't supposed to have liquor, but we had and liberally spiced our Cokes with it. At one point, Gregory, looking up at the airplanes that were continuously passing overhead, said, "How do I know that isn't the Mississippi Air National Guard up there?"

On raised platforms before us the NBC and CBS teams, with ear-phoned spotters, stood with their jackets blowing in the soft, August wind. When a group of Congressmen came in during the middle of a prayer and stopped with heads bowed, Roger Mudd, of CBS, leaned forward with pencil and paper. Marvin Kalb, also of CBS, paced through the crowd gathering Lena Horne, Rev. Fred Shuttlesworth, and Sammy Davis, Jr., for interviews.

When the prayer was over and the people spotted their representatives, like wind leaping up far out on a plain came the chant, "Pass the bill! Pass the bill!" As it moved forward through the ranks, the chant gained strength. "Pass the bill! Pass the bill!" With a sudden, almost embarrassed sigh, it faded and the program continued.

When Martin Luther King, Jr., came up to speak, the quarter million were at fever pitch.

"I have a dream!" M. L. said.

"Tell 'em Martin!" Bob shouted.

"I have a dream!" M. L. said again, and behind us, his voice lost to all but those close to him, a man screamed, "Fuck that dream, Martin! Now, now, goddamit, NOW!"

It had been a day of which America, if it were at all aware of its meaning, could be proud. There had been no time like it before in history, and there would be no time like it again. One could feel the intense desire to surmount the rage of the times. Now, passing along the Lincoln Memorial in a line of traffic, only the tingle of my spine made me know it had been real. How real we have yet to know, for the people had committed, after so long a time, their *bodies* to a given place at a given time.

Groups of far less numbers and far more intent on violence have wrought lasting changes in America; should that group have wrought less, with so much more at stake? Can 250,-000 people, representing millions more, white and black, accept with equanimity what would amount to a resounding slap in the face for their efforts, if the nation failed to respond to the plea made that day?

What was going to happen now?

Millions of people had seen the March on television. Disciplined, determined, the marchers had carried out their aim —to protest the second-class status of the Negro minority. They disappointed those who wished the March to go up in the smoke of violence at the door of the White House. *Now,* what was taking place in the minds of many Americans who saw that display of power, which represented, perhaps, millions of well-wishers who hadn't the money, the time, or the courage to journey to Washington? A display of power begets a display of power. But since the March was conducted along the lines of democratic principles, the opposing power, when it reacted, and it would, would have to remain hidden. Obviously, to be opposed to democratic principles is to be undemocratic. Some social changes have caught us unaware; but this one, I had the feeling as the March ended, would be battled every step of the way. It was clear that social change was the major concern, whether pro or con, of most Americans. Too many people, however, like America as grossly inadequate and crippled as it is, just that way.

I could not bear the silence of the cab, and so I said to the driver, "You'd never believe the March took place, would you?"

"Wasn't that somethin'?" he said, turning to look at me anew. "Were you here?"

"Wouldn't have missed it."

"Wasn't that somethin', an' all the white folks too."

I had found a man to help re-create that day. Wherever I had gone in the country, and when people talked about the March, I dropped in the information that I had taken part in it. Taken part in history.

We have been in this land for seven generations and are descended from the one African in every ten who outlived death, disease, displacement, and degradation. And we, in the person of myself, stood outside the East Gate of the White House. I was not to see the President, but that didn't matter. I, John Alfred Williams, the son of a son of a son of a son of a slave, himself the son of free Africans, was going into the home of Presidents.

There were Negro workmen outside, and as I got out of the cab they stopped to look at me. Who was I?

I knew who I was, and knew how far we had come, and knew we were capable of going the necessary length. Yes, it was rough; yes, people were stupid and bitter and mean and bigoted—some of them, many of them, but, oh, God, I thought, striding up the walk, Ola and John, look at your goddamn boy!

Pushed forward by love and hate and indifference, by history and the increasing pace of it, I stood finally in the office of Schlesinger. He had a large one, and I wondered, as I sat on the long couch, whether it was close to the President or not. A moon-faced man, he did not sit at the desk, but took a chair across from me; a round table between us gave us fencing room. I have mentioned elsewhere that it seemed to me that many times when I went to talk to people, I felt an aura of caution. I felt it again, in the White House. I could see my host weighing things. He is a writer-historian; I am a writer whom he had never read, I'm sure. And there is always something disconcerting about having images shattered without warning. To say that a man is from *Holiday* is to conjure up, almost certainly, the image of a white man. There is no mistaking the current American symbols; they die hard. And thus I saw reflected in his face, I firmly believe, the question from *Hamlet,* "How came he here?" He was astute; he did not try to pigeonhole me as many had: "You on the Negro thing?" "How did they get hold of you?" which means *"Why* did they get hold of you?"

He was leaving the White House, it had been reported, to write a book. He confirmed that report. We were getting our feet wet. We talked briefly about the March and that led into an anecdotal exchange between the late President and Martin Luther King. I had thought that it was Schlesinger who had written something about Eisenhower being a Greek and Kennedy a Roman and that we needed Romans at precisely the time Kennedy took office; he corrected me. It had been columnist Murray Kempton.

There was in that room then, put forth by me, the inevitable question: "What kind of President will Johnson be?"

There were many things he could have said, I imagine, but he chose to say, after selecting his words very carefully, that the new President would be "a conventional American President."

Cautiously, then, we perused civil rights. "It'll be in bad shape if the public-accommodations section, at least, fails to get through."

He meant, we agreed, that the failure of Congress to act quickly and definitely in the passage of the civil-rights package, would result in outbreaks of violence during 1964, more indeed than there had been in 1963.

It was a rather tough interview; no bridges existed between topics, only his silence and his waiting, and behind his nearly opaque glasses, there was a calmness that irritated and frightened me. I talked about what I had felt on the trip and what people had indicated in their discussions with me:

that they no longer award government the confidence they once did.

He looked past me to the window. I, in turn, stared at his bookshelves. He said, "Yes, it seems to be true that people don't give a damn about government."

The interview was over; it had been brief and there had been an interruption. Nothing damns an interview like one party involved in it trying to perceive the reason for its taking place at all.

The trip back to New York, flitting past signs that read: "Get Right With God" "Jesus Saves," "Christ Died for Our Sins." Sitting and thinking, smoking, the search at an end; towns flashing by mantled still with snow; voices drifting up and down the car. Change, I had found it where it most counted, in people, in some people. In these there had been anger at the lengths and sacrifice it took to accomplish change, but all too seldom they had nowhere to turn to help effect it. Fifteen thousand miles and forty states and how many people? I remembered them all and at the times when they spoke the words that most made me remember them.

The sense of ownership, of a vast share in America when I started out? I regained it in Washington, not in the White House, but passing once more along the Mall where I had had a share in history. I had forgotten about it when I began the trip; I had been engrossed to a large extent with myself —a difficult thing in which not to be involved. To be sure there are changes taking place other than social: 40,000 jobs are being eliminated every week because of automation, and we have not yet faced the fact that we do not have, at the moment, the technically trained people to man those machines. To be sure there is growing unrest about our foreign policies, and certainly our long-time "defense" posture creates a mood both belligerent and bewildering. All of these changes in the air have direct relationship to our inability to make a smooth social transition.

I had fear and anger and loneliness in my travels, but, the paradox that is America, there was much love too and goodwill. Perhaps the time will come when in parts of this nation I will not have to fear for my life. When that time comes, a white will not have to fear for his either. We are that intertwined here and now. The challenge is to really look and see how much. And the land still stretches vast and bold. We have only to live up to the challenge of it, and what we have wanted it to be.

America is not everything millions of people wanted it to be and one of the reasons for this is that too few people search for it. Sloth abounds in the land: let the other guy do it. Only a few of us have refused to allow someone other than ourselves to do the jobs or be committed to the search. When I was a child, the fastest aircraft flew at 100 m.p.h., horses were as common as cars, and a man who owned his handtruck could usually find a day's work somewhere. In a little over a quarter of a century all that has been changed. There are many people who have never seen a handtruck, and planes of monstrous size mount the air and take the currents at upwards of 600 m.p.h. Horses have been relegated back to the countrysides. Progress has come pounding down upon us in so many ways, and in other ways it seems not to have touched us at all.

Ours is not a nation deeply rooted in history; we have no temples or pyramids or aqueducts that were built with an unimaginable amount of slave labor. Our glories shall be gained in living up to the ideals we have set for ourselves. Perhaps that is why it is taking so long. It is comparatively easy to chip out and haul away a block of limestone and set it into place. It is not so with people, and I am not ignorant of the fact that much of what we have today was originally based on slave labor or the next thing to it.

What we are faced with today is an alternative: to strive even harder for those credos we set for ourselves or to chip them from our lives altogether. We can no longer do a bit of both; history has seen to that.

I searched and came away with hope. It is there in little pockets. Let it grow; help it grow. I am descended from the one in every ten who survived and somewhere in the continuity of the existences of my forebears I am committed to the search, the hope, the challenge, whether I want to be or not, for America has yet to sing its greatest songs.

AFTERWORD

This afterword is written one year after my trip around America and three months after a four-and-a-half-month trip abroad. Eight consecutive months of travel in 1963 and 1964 was an exhausting stretch.

I returned to this country the day after the three young civil-rights workers disappeared in Mississippi. Mist filled the Narrows and New York Harbor was nearly obscured by those sulky gray clouds that hang about the city on humid days. Liberty was shrouded, as if in sorrow.

That the Civil Rights Act was near passage gave me no joy, for obviously, if the Constitution could not be enforced, then neither could the new laws. They would only become a smoke screen to be blown away before one could get back to the Constitution. Wherever I had gone abroad, in sixteen nations, I found the Congress of the United States held in the greatest contempt. Congress (and America) had divided and joined in combat to decide whether black Americans were citizens of full stature or not. That many of those foreign nations had pressing problems of their own in no way reduced the contempt; their problems were of another kind.

I felt upon my return that I had changed, perhaps even grown. The change or growth had commenced in September, 1963, when I started the trip around the United States. The process, as I indicated in the foreword, had been costly. I had had to reach the conclusion that man, as I knew him best, in America, was not basically good, as is always suggested, but evil in the primitive, possessive, and destructive sense. I knew good people existed; I had been fortunate in meeting many of them. But stack American upon American, reach into the heap and pull one out, and the chances of getting hold of one who measured up to the ideal American we all would like to be would be practically nil.

This is not strange in the light of the American past. We were thieves and murderers, many of us. We had to be whipped out of filthy European jails and forced aboard flimsy vessels to journey here, many of us. Some of us came indentured into slavery beyond belief, beyond, yes, even the living death that was Negro slavery. Some of us survived pogroms and warfare between lesser nobles. Some of us ran out of rice or potatoes; for some of us no green graced the rocks of Sicily or Greece. On the run, only the strong survive. We were a strong people.

From the beginning Americans defied the natural laws of territory and possession, and in the process eliminated from coast to coast and from North to South, almost an entire race of people, the American Indian. For the free land offered to many of us in the West, we hocked everything (there was not much on the crowded eastern seaboard—the American industrial revolution was but a primitive step toward the automation we now face) and raced to take up that free acreage. We were born of violence.

Having finally accepted this most logical conclusion, for it does explain not only our own history but that of the world, I dug into my apartment, hung up the mementos of my travels, and sat down to work on a new novel. It was about ten days before the publication of Part I of the *Holiday* articles. After that, the mail started to come. In the beginning some of the letters had no return address, so I knew even before I opened them what those writers had to say. I was once again struck by the stupidity of the American bigot who often cloaks himself in Fundamentalist righteousness. His clichés, ripped bodily from the racial myths, were scrawled in illiterate passages.

But most of the letters were warm. Many writers sought advice. The ages ranged from seventeen to eighty. There was a measure of panic in all the letters. People wanted to know what to do to help America in its crisis. I answered every one saying what I could, but I knew it was never enough. I don't know anymore what will be enough to keep us from going over the brink. That is precisely what the letter writers were afraid of, even if they didn't spell it out. I think that the impression I got while on the trip, that the people no longer have confidence in their government, is even more valid now than it was a year ago.

Generally, I think, we are drawing closer and closer to offering a vote of no confidence in government. We depend on it for many things that it never delivers. It has become a business; it is the largest single employer in history. It simply cannot be objective. Half the time we do not know what it is up to. Its police agencies, especially in the area of civil rights, have put forth a sorry record indeed.

I feel that the murder of Kennedy and several other key, though lesser-known people, and the upsurging civil-rights movement, the plunging deterioration of both the Republican and Democratic parties are but the coincidental aspects of a future toward which we have been stumbling all the time. The result is that grim anarchy is but one crisis away, perhaps two, from overwhelming the land.

We have been given shock after shock—kids bombed to pieces, highway drivers and hitchhikers blasted by shotguns, leaders great and small obliterated by high-powered rifles, example upon example of police collusion; there are so many hands in the public till that they can no longer be counted. For close to forty years we've had a bureau to combat narcotics addiction, but despite the furor over the danger of cancer in smoking legal cigarettes, few persons indeed have dared to mention nicotine addiction.

We are at peace with former enemies who, with a bit more luck in World War II, would be sharing this nation between them. Today, with the help of the U.S. dollar, they rank in prosperity close to our own. Only the dead who fought against them don't know how it is now.

DOESN'T ANYONE GET STINKING MAD ABOUT ANYTHING ANY MORE?

That man is descended from the killer ape is fact. We aren't too eager to know that, however. Knowing where we came from, we should be able to chart a better course for ourselves. Reason, we keep telling ourselves with undue pride, separates us from the lesser animals. But we have not used all the reason at our command. We refuse to, or we are never taught how to. Thus we stand with our feet in feces and our head in the stars, oblivious to the paradox. I am afraid that the worst is still to come.

The worst must come because we cannot have laws that are not enforced. Nor can we have laws that protect the rich and expose the poor just because the two classes live in that most primitive of conflicts between the haves and the have-nots.

If we are to avoid the worst, we must find a way, each of us, to partake completely in the selection of honest and concerned men to represent us in the Congress of the United States. Personally, I do not think there are many men of such caliber in Washington at the moment. We must also be as diligent in our search for men to fill the lesser offices of state, county, and city. Public services must be clarified. It must no longer mean being in charge of people, but serving them. For too many, public office has become merely a position that offers a good income. It is no wonder that, with the passage of time, our Presidents have tended to be millionaires, people who do not have to use the office to make an income.

I have not written specifically about the "Negro Revolution." Everything that affects America affects the Negro. Perhaps even truer is the fact that everything that affects the Negro affects America. All the relevant words, facts, and ideas have been set down. I have nothing new to add. Except that I now know that a great majority of white people have no intention of sharing with black people what we have called the American dream—unless they are forced to. Since the democratic process works slowly, we can assume that they are not going to be forced to immediately. Yet the inequalities that exist in this land could be done away with overnight if conscientious citizens could become involved in responsible government. As matters stand now, small groups of men select candidates; we only vote on their choices. And under present conditions all Negroes must soon realize that they will be given nothing until they demand it and, if necessary, fight for it.

I have been to Africa and know that it is not my home. America is; it is my country too, and has been for generations. As I said, I am committed to the search for its true meaning; I hope what I have found is not it. I am forced to hope for it and I have no choice but to meet the challenge of it. Yes, it is true that America has yet to sing its greatest songs, but it had better hurry up and find the key to the tunes.

Other SIGNET and MENTOR Books
of Related Interest

THE THIRD GENERATION   **by Chester Himes**

The searing novel of a woman who passes for white, and, raging against her Negro heritage, brings ruin to her family.   (#T2532—75¢)

WHEN THE WORD IS GIVEN   **by Louis E. Lomax**

An eye-opening account of the Black Muslims in America, and of their late leader, Malcolm X. By the author of *The Negro Revolt*.   (#P2429—60¢)

SKIN DEEP   **by Ralph G. Martin**

A compelling and timely novel about the lives of four Negroes who seek freedom and happiness in Paris.   (#P2777—60¢)

THE NEGRO REVOLT   **by Louis E. Lomax**

A Negro writer's blunt, brilliant report on the current racial unrest in America.   (#T2273—75¢)

THE TROUBLESOME PRESENCE
      by Eli Ginzberg and Alfred S. Eichner

A comprehensive history of the Negro's struggle for equality from colonial days to the present time, a study of the background of "sit-ins," "kneel-downs," and "freedom rides."   (#MT667—75¢)

THE PRIMITIVE   **by Chester Himes**

A forthright novel about a tragic love affair between two self-destructive people—a white woman and a Negro man whose lives had placed them on the fringes of society.   (#P2595—60¢)

NATIVE SON   **by Richard Wright**

The stark, moving novel about a young Negro's self-destructive efforts to find freedom through acts of violence.   (#T2598—75¢)

GO TELL IT ON THE MOUNTAIN   **by James Baldwin**

The brilliant first novel by the author of the bestseller, *Another Country*. Set in New York's Harlem.   (#P2272—60¢)

Other SIGNET Books on Current Affairs

THE BRAIN WATCHERS   **by Martin L. Gross**

A full-scale expose of the multimillion-dollar psychological testing industry and the use—and misuse—of "personality tests" in business.   (#T2382—75¢)

IN THE MIDST OF PLENTY: The Poor in America
                                   by Ben H. Bagdikian

A noted journalist records the painful stories of America's poor in an eloquent plea for an all-out attack on poverty.
                                   (#P2535—60¢)

RICH MAN, POOR MAN   **by Herman P. Miller**

Reasons and remedies for the distressing income gap that exists today in an affluent America. Based on recent U. S. census figures. Introduction by Willard Wirtz.
                                   (#T2635—75¢)

SLUMS AND SUBURBS   **by James B. Conant**

The distinguished former President of Harvard University attacks the inequalities that exist between the public schools of the slums and those of the wealthy suburbs.
                                   (#P2421—60¢)

THE WASTED AMERICANS   **by Edgar May**

A Pulitzer Prize-winning journalist explains why billions spent on relief have failed to help America's permanent poor.   (#P2603—60¢)

AMERICA TOMORROW: Creating the Great Society
                         by the Staff of *The New Republic*

This paperback reprint of *The New Republic's* twenty-fifth anniversary issue explores the major areas in American life destined to benefit by future progress.
                                   (#P2667—60¢)

THE GREAT TREASURY RAID   **by Philip M. Stern**

A blasting report on the abuses of America's tax laws with constructive proposals for revamping them on a more equitable structure.   (#T2609—75¢)